W9-CER-128

THE PHYSICALLY CHALLENGED

GENERAL EDITORS

Dale C. Garell, M.D.
Medical Director, California Children Services, Department of Health Services,
   County of Los Angeles
Associate Dean for Curriculum; Clinical Professor, Department of Pediatrics &
   Family Medicine, University of Southern California School of Medicine
Former President, Society for Adolescent Medicine

Solomon H. Snyder, M.D.
Distinguished Service Professor of Neuroscience, Pharmacology, and Psychiatry, Johns
   Hopkins University School of Medicine
Former President, Society for Neuroscience
Albert Lasker Award in Medical Research, 1978

CONSULTING EDITORS

Robert W. Blum, M.D., Ph.D.
Professor and Director, Division of General Pediatrics and Adolescent Health,
   University of Minnesota

Charles E. Irwin, Jr., M.D.
Professor of Pediatrics; Director, Division of Adolescent Medicine, University of California, San Francisco

Lloyd J. Kolbe, Ph.D.
Director of the Division of Adolescent and School Health, Center for Chronic
   Disease Prevention and Health Promotion, Centers for Disease Control

Jordan J. Popkin
Former Director, Division of Federal Employee Occupational Health, U.S. Public
   Health Service Region I

Joseph L. Rauh, M.D.
Professor of Pediatrics and Medicine, Adolescent Medicine, Children's Hospital
   Medical Center, Cincinnati
Former President, Society for Adolescent Medicine

THE ENCYCLOPEDIA OF
HEALTH

MEDICAL DISORDERS AND THEIR TREATMENT

Dale C. Garell, M.D. · General Editor

THE PHYSICALLY CHALLENGED

Don Nardo

Introduction by C. Everett Koop, M.D., Sc.D.

former Surgeon General, U. S. Public Health Service

CHELSEA HOUSE PUBLISHERS

New York · Philadelphia

The goal of the ENCYCLOPEDIA OF HEALTH *is to provide general information in the ever-changing areas of physiology, psychology, and related medical issues. The titles in this series are not intended to take the place of the professional advice of a physician or other health care professional.*

CHELSEA HOUSE PUBLISHERS
EDITORIAL DIRECTOR   Richard Rennert
EXECUTIVE MANAGING EDITOR   Karyn Gullen Browne
COPY CHIEF   Robin James
PICTURE EDITOR   Adrian G. Allen
ART DIRECTOR   Robert Mitchell
MANUFACTURING DIRECTOR   Gerald Levine

The Encyclopedia of Health
SENIOR EDITOR   Don Nardo

Staff for THE PHYSICALLY CHALLENGED
EDITORIAL ASSISTANT   Mary B. Sisson
PICTURE RESEARCHER   Sandy Jones
DESIGNER   M. Cambraia Magalhães

First Printing
1   3   5   7   9   8   6   4   2

Library of Congress Cataloging-in-Publication Data
Nardo, Don, 1947–
    The physically challenged / Don Nardo.
        p. cm.—(The Encyclopedia of health. Medical disorders and their treatment)
    Includes bibliographical references and index.
ISBN 0-7910-0073-7.
        0-7910-0500-3 (pbk.)
    1. Physically handicapped—Juvenile literature. [1. Physically handicapped] I. Title.
II. Series.   93-26206
HV3011.N27 1994   CIP
362.4—dc20   AC

CONTENTS

THE ENCYCLOPEDIA OF
H E A L T H

THE HEALTHY BODY

The Circulatory System
Dental Health
The Digestive System
The Endocrine System
Exercise
Genetics & Heredity
The Human Body: An Overview
Hygiene
The Immune System
Memory & Learning
The Musculoskeletal System
The Nervous System
Nutrition
The Reproductive System
The Respiratory System
The Senses
Sleep
Speech & Hearing
Sports Medicine
Vision
Vitamins & Minerals

THE LIFE CYCLE

Adolescence
Adulthood
Aging
Childhood
Death & Dying
The Family
Friendship & Love
Pregnancy & Birth

MEDICAL ISSUES

Careers in Health Care
Environmental Health
Folk Medicine
Health Care Delivery
Holistic Medicine
Medical Ethics
Medical Fakes & Frauds
Medical Technology
Medicine & the Law
Occupational Health
Public Health

PSYCHOLOGICAL DISORDERS AND THEIR TREATMENT

Anxiety & Phobias
Child Abuse
Compulsive Behavior
Delinquency & Criminal Behavior
Depression
Diagnosing & Treating Mental Illness
Eating Habits & Disorders
Learning Disabilities
Mental Retardation
Personality Disorders
Schizophrenia
Stress Management
Suicide

MEDICAL DISORDERS AND THEIR TREATMENT

AIDS
Allergies
Alzheimer's Disease
Arthritis
Birth Defects
Cancer
The Common Cold
Diabetes
Emergency Medicine
Gynecological Disorders
Headaches
The Hospital
Kidney Disorders
Medical Diagnosis
The Mind-Body Connection
Mononucleosis and Other Infectious Diseases
Nuclear Medicine
Organ Transplants
Pain
The Physically Challenged
Poisons & Toxins
Prescription & OTC Drugs
Sexually Transmitted Diseases
Skin Disorders
Stroke & Heart Disease
Substance Abuse
Tropical Medicine

PREVENTION AND EDUCATION: THE KEYS TO GOOD HEALTH

C. Everett Koop, M.D., Sc.D.
former Surgeon General,
U.S. Public Health Service

The issue of health education has received particular attention in recent years because of the presence of AIDS in the news. But our response to this particular tragedy points up a number of broader issues that doctors, public health officials, educators, and the public face. In particular, it points up the necessity for sound health education for citizens of all ages.

Over the past 25 years this country has been able to bring about dramatic declines in the death rates for heart disease, stroke, accidents, and for people under the age of 45, cancer. Today, Americans generally eat better and take better care of themselves than ever before. Thus, with the help of modern science and technology, they have a better chance of surviving serious—even catastrophic—illnesses. That's the good news.

But, like every phonograph record, there's a flip side, and one with special significance for young adults. According to a report issued in 1979 by Dr. Julius Richmond, my predecessor as Surgeon General, Americans aged 15 to 24 had a higher death rate in 1979 than they did 20 years earlier. The causes: violent death and injury, alcohol and drug abuse, unwanted pregnancies, and sexually transmitted diseases. Adolescents are particularly vulnerable because they are beginning to explore their own sexuality and perhaps to experiment with drugs. The need for educating young people is critical, and the price of neglect is high.

Yet even for the population as a whole, our health is still far from what it could be. Why? A 1974 Canadian government report attributed all death and disease to four broad elements: inadequacies in the health care system, behavioral factors or unhealthy life-styles, environmental hazards, and human biological factors.

To be sure, there are diseases that are still beyond the control of even our advanced medical knowledge and techniques. And despite yearnings that are as old as the human race itself, there is no "fountain of youth" to ward off aging and death. Still, there is a solution to many of the problems that undermine sound health. In a word, that solution is prevention. Prevention, which includes health promotion and education, saves lives, improves the quality of life, and in the long run, saves money.

In the United States, organized public health activities and preventive medicine have a long history. Important milestones in this country or foreign breakthroughs adopted in the United States include the improvement of sanitary procedures and the development of pasteurized milk in the late 19th century and the introduction in the mid-20th century of effective vaccines against polio, measles, German measles, mumps, and other once-rampant diseases. Internationally, organized public health efforts began on a wide-scale basis with the International Sanitary Conference of 1851, to which 12 nations sent representatives. The World Health Organization, founded in 1948, continues these efforts under the aegis of the United Nations, with particular emphasis on combating communicable diseases and the training of health care workers.

Despite these accomplishments, much remains to be done in the field of prevention. For too long, we have had a medical care system that is science- and technology-based, focused, essentially, on illness and mortality. It is now patently obvious that both the social and the economic costs of such a system are becoming insupportable.

Implementing prevention—and its corollaries, health education and pro-motion—is the job of several groups of people.

First, the medical and scientific professions need to continue basic scientific research, and here we are making considerable progress. But increased concern with prevention will also have a decided impact on how primary care doctors practice medicine. With a shift to health-based rather than morbidity-based medicine, the role of the "new physician" will include a healthy dose of patient education.

Second, practitioners of the social and behavioral sciences—psychologists, economists, city planners—along with lawyers, business leaders, and government officials—must solve the practical and ethical dilemmas confronting us: poverty, crime, civil rights, literacy, education, employment, housing, sanitation, environmental protection, health care delivery systems, and so forth. All of these issues affect public health.

Third is the public at large. We'll consider that very important group in a moment.

Fourth, and the linchpin in this effort, is the public health profession—doctors, epidemiologists, teachers—who must harness the professional expertise of the first two groups and the common sense and cooperation of the third, the public. They must define the problems statistically and qualitatively and then help us set priorities for finding the solutions.

To a very large extent, improving those statistics is the responsibility of every individual. So let's consider more specifically what the role of the individual should be and why health education is so important to that role. First, and most obvious, individuals can protect themselves from illness and injury and thus minimize their need for professional medical care. They can eat nutritious food; get adequate exercise; avoid tobacco, alcohol, and drugs; and take prudent steps to avoid accidents. The proverbial "apple a day keeps the doctor away" is not so far from the truth, after all.

Second, individuals should actively participate in their own medical care. They should schedule regular medical and dental checkups. Should they develop an illness or injury, they should know when to treat themselves and when to seek professional help. To gain the maximum benefit from any medical treatment that they do require, individuals must become partners in that treatment. For instance, they should understand the effects and side effects of medications. I counsel young physicians that there is no such thing as too much information when talking with patients. But the corollary is the patient must know enough about the nuts and bolts of the healing process to understand what the doctor is telling him or her. That is at least partially the patient's responsibility.

Education is equally necessary for us to understand the ethical and public policy issues in health care today. Sometimes individuals will encounter these issues in making decisions about their own treatment or that of family members. Other citizens may encounter them as jurors in medical malpractice cases. But we all become involved, indirectly, when we elect our public officials, from school board members to the president. Should surrogate parenting be legal? To what extent is drug testing desirable, legal, or necessary? Should there be public funding for family planning, hospitals, various types of medical research, and other medical care for the indigent? How should we allocate scant technological resources, such as kidney dialysis and organ transplants? What is the proper role of government in protecting the rights of patients?

What are the broad goals of public health in the United States today? In 1980, the Public Health Service issued a report aptly entitled *Promoting Health—Preventing Disease: Objectives for the Nation.* This report expressed its goals in terms of mortality and in terms of intermediate goals in education and health improvement. It identified 15 major concerns: controlling high blood pressure; improving family planning; improving pregnancy care and infant health; increasing the rate of immunization; controlling sexually transmitted diseases; controlling the presence of toxic agents and radiation in the environment; improving occupational safety and health; preventing accidents; promoting water fluoridation and dental health; controlling infectious diseases; decreasing smoking; decreasing alcohol and drug abuse; improving nutrition; promoting physical fitness and exercise; and controlling stress and violent behavior.

For healthy adolescents and young adults (ages 15 to 24), the specific goal was a 20% reduction in deaths, with a special focus on motor vehicle injuries and alcohol and drug abuse. For adults (ages 25 to 64), the aim was 25% fewer deaths, with a concentration on heart attacks, strokes, and cancers.

Smoking is perhaps the best example of how individual behavior can have a direct impact on health. Today, cigarette smoking is recognized as the single most important preventable cause of death in our society. It is responsible for more cancers and more cancer deaths than any other known agent; is a prime risk factor for heart and blood vessel disease, chronic bronchitis, and emphysema; and is a frequent cause of complications in pregnancies and of babies born prematurely, underweight, or with potentially fatal respiratory and cardiovascular problems.

Since the release of the Surgeon General's first report on smoking in 1964, the proportion of adult smokers has declined substantially, from 43% in 1965 to 30.5% in 1985. Since 1965, 37 million people have quit smoking. Although there is still much work to be done if we are to become a "smoke-free society," it is heartening to note that public health and public education efforts—such as warnings on cigarette packages and bans on broadcast advertising—have already had significant effects.

In 1835, Alexis de Tocqueville, a French visitor to America, wrote, "In America the passion for physical well-being is general." Today, as then, health and fitness are front-page items. But with the greater scientific and technological resources now available to us, we are in a far stronger position to make good health care available to everyone. And with the greater technological threats to us as we approach the 21st century, the need to do so is more urgent than ever before. Comprehensive information about basic biology, preventive medicine, medical and surgical treatments, and related ethical and public policy issues can help you arm yourself with the knowledge you need to be healthy throughout your life.

FOREWORD

Dale C. Garell, M.D.

Advances in our understanding of health and disease during the 20th century have been truly remarkable. Indeed, it could be argued that modern health care is one of the greatest accomplishments in all of human history. In the early 20th century, improvements in sanitation, water treatment, and sewage disposal reduced death rates and increased longevity. Previously untreatable illnesses can now be managed with antibiotics, immunizations, and modern surgical techniques. Discoveries in the fields of immunology, genetic diagnosis, and organ transplantation are revolutionizing the prevention and treatment of disease. Modern medicine is even making inroads against cancer and heart disease, two of the leading causes of death in the United States.

Although there is much to be proud of, medicine continues to face enormous challenges. Science has vanquished diseases such as smallpox and polio, but new killers, most notably AIDS, confront us. Moreover, we now victimize ourselves with what some have called "diseases of choice," or those brought on by drug and alcohol abuse, bad eating habits, and mismanagement of the stresses and strains of contemporary life. The very technology that is doing so much to prolong life has brought with it previously unimaginable ethical dilemmas related to issues of death and dying. The rising cost of health care is a matter of central concern to us all. And violence in the form of automobile accidents, homicide, and suicide remains the major killer of young adults.

In the past, most people were content to leave health care and medical treatment in the hands of professionals. But since the 1960s, the consumer of medical care—that is, the patient—has assumed an increasingly central role in the management of his or her own health. There has also been a new emphasis placed on prevention: People are recognizing that their own actions can help prevent many of the conditions that have caused death and disease in the past. This accounts for the growing commitment to good nutrition and regular exercise, for the increasing number of people who are choosing not to smoke, and for a new moderation in people's drinking habits.

People want to know more about themselves and their own health. They are curious about their body: its anatomy, physiology, and biochemistry. They want to keep up with rapidly evolving medical technologies and procedures. They are willing to educate themselves about common disorders and diseases so that they can be full partners in their own health care.

THE ENCYCLOPEDIA OF HEALTH is designed to provide the basic knowledge that readers will need if they are to take significant responsibility for their own health. It is also meant to serve as a frame of reference for further study and exploration. The encyclopedia is divided into five subsections: The Healthy Body; The Life Cycle; Medical Disorders & Their Treatment; Psychological Disorders & Their Treatment; and Medical Issues. For each topic covered by the encyclopedia, we present the essential facts about the relevant biology; the symptoms, diagnosis, and treatment of common diseases and disorders; and ways in which you can prevent or reduce the severity of health problems when that is possible. The encyclopedia also projects what may lie ahead in the way of future treatment or prevention strategies.

The broad range of topics and issues covered in the encyclopedia reflects that human health encompasses physical, psychological, social, environmental, and spiritual well-being. Just as the mind and the body are inextricably linked, so, too, is the individual an integral part of the wider world that comprises his or her family, society, and environment. To discuss health in its broadest aspect it is necessary to explore the many ways in which it is connected to such fields as law, social science, public policy, economics, and even religion. And so, the encyclopedia is meant to be a bridge between science, medical technology, the world at large, and you. I hope that it will inspire you to pursue in greater depth particular areas of interest and that you will take advantage of the suggestions for further reading and the lists of resources and organizations that can provide additional information.

CHAPTER 1

FROM AN
INSENSITIVE PAST

The actor Jack Klugman poses with some youngsters suffering from Down's syndrome.

The *physically challenged* are those persons who have physical defects or disorders that keep them from performing some of the everyday tasks and activities others of their age routinely perform. According to writer and educator Gilda Berger, "They may lack the ability to control parts of their body. They may be missing a limb. They may have complete or partial loss of vision or of hearing. Their heart, lungs, muscles, bones, or nervous system may be diseased, damaged, or deformed. They may have an incurable illness." Such physical challenges range from different degrees of blindness and deafness; to crippling conditions such as _muscular dystrophy, cerebral palsy,_ and various kinds of paralysis; to disfigurements caused by accidents.

No one knows for sure how many people living in the United States are physically challenged. Medical authorities estimate that well over half a million people require wheelchairs to get around and that between three and four million more need to use crutches, braces, or canes regularly. Perhaps three million Americans are deaf, with another twelve million having lesser but still serious hearing impairments. And as many as two million people are blind, with between eight and nine million more having various degrees of visual impairment. In addition, at least two million people are homebound because of long-term diseases and disorders, and at any one time as many as thirteen million people have temporary serious injuries such as back injuries, broken limbs, and severe burns. That means that at least forty million people in the United States, or one person in six, face some kind of physical challenge that significantly affects their lives. When one considers the fact that the life of each physically challenged person touches many other lives—those of family, friends, co-workers, and medical caregivers—it becomes clear that nearly everyone in society is touched or affected in some way by such physical challenges.

Worries About Words

The term "physically challenged" is a relatively new one. In prior centuries, when society as a whole was less understanding of and sympathetic to physical impairments, people with such challenges were called "halting," "lame," "cripples," and other negative terms, often in a derogatory manner. In the 20th century, with widespread advances in the medical and social sciences, the more humane terms "disabled" and "handicapped" came into general use. In the 1980s many people began to feel that these terms too had become somewhat outdated. They pointed out that the words "handicap" and "disability" might have negative connotations because they imply that someone cannot do something, such as participate in a routine, everyday activity. And it is very important for everyone, no matter what their physical condition, not to feel limited, restricted, or left out of the mainstream of everyday life. According to this view, the word "challenge," defined as a stimulating or interesting task or problem, implies unlimited possibilities and is, therefore, much more positive and optimistic.

As a result, more and more people—in literature, on TV and radio, and in public speeches—are beginning to use the term "physically challenged." This book is no exception. However, because many of the books, articles, personal accounts, and other references on this topic

This 1853 engraving shows prosthetic devices made by Palmer & Company, which won medals for the "best artificial limb" at an industrial exhibition. Soon the Civil War would make this a very profitable line of business.

retain the terms "disabled" and "handicapped," these words also appear in this volume. In this context, they should not be thought of as having any negative connotation, but rather as being interchangeable with the term "physically challenged."

Interestingly, it is often people who are not physically challenged who are most worried about what to call people who are. A majority of people with physical disabilities want to be treated like everyone else and are not as sensitive about the use of words as many people suppose they are. This applies to many common expressions used in everyday speech, phrases that some people may assume are inappropriate in certain situations. As medical writers Charlene DeLoach and Bobby Greer put it in their book *Adjustment to Severe Physical Disability:*

> When interacting with the disabled, many persons feel they are committing . . . social "no-no's" if they "slip" and use expressions such as "See what I mean" with someone who may be blind. Another example would be, "Let's run over and get something to eat" when speaking to someone who is in a wheelchair. To the naive person, that would on the surface be extremely insensitive. In certain cases, within specific contexts, it may be. But in the majority of instances where expressions such as these are used, they pass for everyday expressions with no belittling intent on the part of the speaker. In actuality, if no such intent is present, the use of these expressions by a non-disabled person speaking with a disabled person is quite a compliment to the latter! It indicates that the speaker feels comfortable with the individual and does not consider her [or him] first and foremost a disabled person.

In general, the words to avoid when referring to the physically challenged are those that have obvious negative connotations, such as victim, sufferer, afflicted, wheelchair-bound, and restricted. All of these suggest that the person being described is to be pitied or treated differently than other people. People who are physically challenged want neither pity nor special treatment. As already stated, they want to be treated the same way as nonchallenged people. It is important, then, to learn not to refer to nonchallenged persons as "normal," since that implies that challenged persons are somehow abnormal.

Killed or Left Out To Die

It might seem that an unusual amount of attention is paid to sensitive and positive word use in relation to the physically challenged. But in light of past events, such attention is certainly understandable. The unfortunate fact is that widespread sensitive and humane treatment of people with various kinds of disabilities is a relatively new phenomenon. Throughout most of history, nearly all physically challenged people were treated cruelly, unfairly, and unjustly by societies that were ignorant about both the causes and proper treatments of physical problems.

The earliest, most primitive human societies, consisting of hunter-gatherers, were especially cruel to people who were born with or later acquired physical handicaps. In these societies, the very survival of a

Today many efforts are made to ease the special circumstances of the physically challenged, such as providing guaranteed parking spaces near work or shopping.

tribe depended on each person contributing in some way. Among these contributions were hunting for food, fighting in battles against other tribes, and fulfilling everyday village duties. In the eyes of tribal leaders, people with physical disabilities could make no such contributions. And the able-bodied had neither the time nor the skills to care for them. Disabled people were, therefore, considered to be a burden on society. Disabled people were also seen as having been deformed or even possessed by evil spirits. It is not surprising, then, that children born with physical disfigurements were immediately killed. And anyone who became physically handicapped later in life was either killed or driven away. According to an old European account that described traditional, ancient tribal practices, "Old and weak parents were killed by the son. Blind, squinting, and deformed children were disposed of by the father, either by the sword, drowning, or burning. Lame and blind servants were hanged to trees."

Later societies carried on some of these cruel treatments of the physically disabled. The early Hebrews believed that physical defor-

This ancient Egyptian stone carving shows a man with an atrophied right foot, perhaps caused by infantile paralysis.

mities were the result of God punishing sinners for evil acts or thoughts. Luckily, the Hebrews developed laws that forbade the killing of blind, deaf, or deformed persons. But society still viewed such persons as moral, as well as physical, outcasts and shunned them. Except in unusual cases, blind and crippled people were reduced to begging for coins in the streets in order to stay alive.

The Greeks, who were in many ways the most socially and politically advanced people of ancient times, were at the same time backward and unjust in their treatment of disabled people. In the Greek city-state of Sparta, deformed infants were either killed or exposed, that is, left outside to die of exposure. In Athens, another city-state, one early practice was to kill deformed, or "imperfect," babies by placing them in clay containers.

The Romans regularly exposed infants for a number of reasons, including physical deformity. The Roman writer Seneca defended this practice as reasonable, saying, "What is good must be set apart from what is good for nothing." Both the rich and poor in Rome practiced death by exposure and for this reason the proportion of disabled people in Roman society was much lower than in modern society. There were *some* disabled Romans, as well as disabled Greeks, however, because not all exposed babies died. In both Greece and Rome some people actually searched for foundling infants, whom they raised either as their own children or as household slaves. Historian Lionel Casson writes in his book *Daily Life in Ancient Rome:*

> Some of the most famous tales of ancient literature, such as the story of Oedipus or of Romulus and Remus, concern infants who were exposed and then rescued in the nick of time, and there are even a few important historical figures who started life this way. As a matter of fact, people found it profitable to be on the lookout for foundlings in order to raise them as slaves either for their own household or for sale. In Roman Egypt, and very likely elsewhere as well, they scavenged for them in the town dump, where it was the practice to abandon infants; in legal documents slaves are frequently designated as being "from the dump."

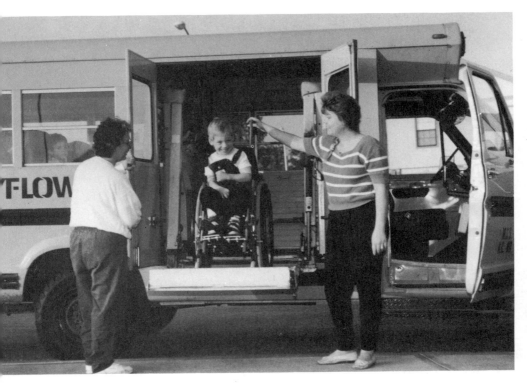

This young boy suffers from cerebral palsy, but he can count on special bus transportation to get him to school.

In this way, some disabled people rejected by ancient societies survived, although most that did led bleak, hopeless lives as slaves.

From Dependence to Independence

During medieval times, from about 400 to 1500 A.D., the situation for disabled people was no better. Physically deformed and handicapped people, as well as those with long-term disfiguring diseases and conditions such as leprosy and *spina bifida,* were considered to be cursed by God or actually possessed by Satan. Such people were often verbally abused, beaten, stoned, or forced to live apart from the rest of society. People who possessed marked physical differences from the "norm," such as dwarfs and hunchbacks, often became the target of cruel humor when kings and other nobles enlisted them as court jesters to entertain guests. Yet among society's disabled, the jesters were, in a way, the lucky ones. Many others, especially deformed women, were persecuted as witches. Among the tens of thousands of people in Europe who were imprisoned, tortured, hung, drowned, and burned at the stake as witches during the period from about 1250 to 1600, many were those whose crime consisted merely of being physically impaired in some way.

Although the idea that disabled people were possessed by evil spirits or by Satan began to lose credence in the 1500s when great new scientific strides were being made in Europe, religion often continued to perpetuate old stereotypes about the physically disabled. Gilda Berger explains that John Calvin, the French religious leader,

> set back the cause of the disabled. In his Christian creed, now known as Calvinism, he stated that originally man was created perfect and pure in the image of God. Men and women who were not perfect and pure (such as the disabled) showed that they had fallen out of grace with God. The only way to be saved [Calvin advocated] is through the grace of God. Good works or good deeds are of no help in achieving salvation. This view added another burden to the lives of the disabled.

The disabled fared a bit better in colonial America during the 1600s and 1700s, when a majority of people actually showed them some compassion. However, people with physical problems of one kind or another were still looked upon as burdens on their families and on society in general. It was taken for granted that disabled people could not become independent, useful members of society. So family members or the government supported them and kept them in dependent, largely restricted situations. Occasionally there were exceptions to this rule, as in the cases of a few disabled people who rose to prominent positions in society. As Berger points out, Peter Stuyvesant, the first governor of the Dutch colony of New Amsterdam, later called New York, had a wooden peg leg, the result of losing a leg in battle. And Stephen Hopkins, one of the signers of the U.S. Declaration of Inde-

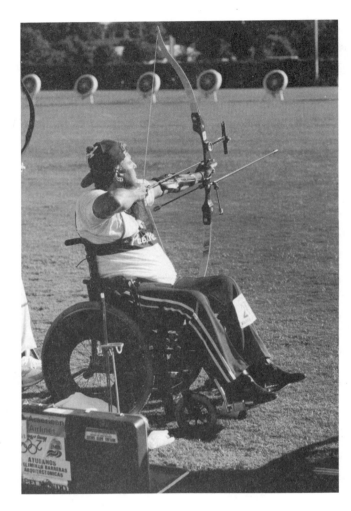

A disabled veteran practices archery.

pendence, had cerebral palsy, a condition that caused his hands and other body parts to shake uncontrollably. It is important to point out, however, that at the time these and other disabled persons of distinction had the benefit of being white and male in a culture completely dominated by white males. Disabled women, blacks, and other minorities had no chance of becoming independent and gaining recognition.

Not until the 1800s did attitudes and customs regarding the disabled begin to change significantly, and this was mainly in the cases of the blind and the deaf. In 1832 in Boston, Samuel Gridley Howe estab-

Modern prosthetic devices use advanced designs and materials, and the people using them can enjoy many athletic activities without awkwardness.

lished the first school for the blind, which later became known as the Perkins Institute. One of his students, Laura Bridgman, a young girl who had lost her sight at the age of two, became a national celebrity when Howe taught her to write and communicate. Helen Keller, who was both blind and deaf, and who also became a celebrity when she overcame these challenges, was a later attendee of the Perkins Institute.

In 1817, teacher Thomas Hopkins Gallaudet, believing that deaf people could learn to lead useful, fulfilling lives, founded the Hartford School for the Deaf in Hartford, Connecticut. His son Edward established Gallaudet College, dedicated exclusively to educating people with hearing impairments, in Washington, D.C., in 1864. The Gallaudets stressed the use of sign language and showed that deaf people could indeed become useful members of society.

The work of Howe, the Gallaudets, and other educational pioneers, as well as the courage, hard work, and ultimate success of many of their students, inspired others. This, along with the advent of new medical knowledge, led to the 20th century's universally more humane attitudes toward the physically challenged. These factors also made it possible, for the first time in history, for physically challenged people to look forward to safe, productive, dignified, and happy lives.

CHAPTER 2

SOME COMMON CHALLENGES

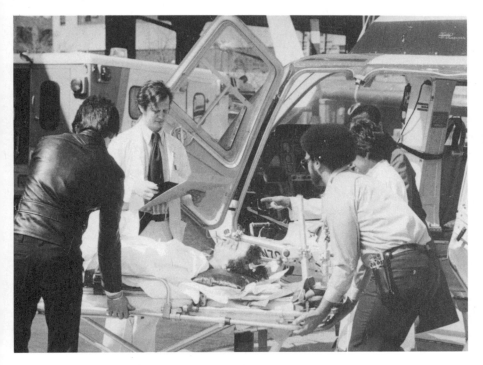

Not all physical disabilities appear at birth. Accidental injuries are one of the most common and preventable causes of physical disabilities.

In order to understand and appreciate what life for physically challenged people is like, it is first essential to understand the nature of the daunting challenges they face. Physical challenges fall into three general categories. The first category consists of physical conditions people are born with. Some babies are born without sight or hearing, for example, while others have defective hearts, deformed arms or legs, or missing bones. Still others lack control of their muscles due to conditions such as cerebral palsy, or have brain disorders that cause difficulty in speaking or epileptic seizures. This category of challenges also includes *genetic*, or inherited, diseases and disorders, such as *hemophilia* and muscular dystrophy.

The second kind of physical challenge is caused by disease. For instance, severe eye or ear infections can lead to blindness or deafness. And *arthritis* can deform the joints and make many average physical activities painful or impossible. Some diseases, such as polio and *meningitis*, can lead to paralysis. And heart disease and diabetes often severely limit normal physical activity.

The third type of physical challenge results from accidents. Every year, thousands of people are seriously injured in accidents that occur in the home, at work, at the beach, and in automobiles and other modes of transportation. Many of these injuries, including severe burns, crushed spines, and damaged eyes and brains, can permanently disfigure or incapacitate people.

Loss of Sight

Blindness is one of the most common physical challenges, and its causes fall into all three challenge categories. Some babies are born totally or partially blind. About one out of every 5,000 children is born with serious vision impairment. Donald J. Meyer, author of *Living with a Brother or Sister with Special Needs*, explains,

> When babies are born with vision problems, they have what is called a *congenital* vision problem. Sometimes it may be caused by an infection that the mother had during her pregnancy, such as German measles. Some forms of vision loss are inherited, and can be passed from the parents to the child. If a child inherits a vision loss, the parents may also have a vision loss, or they may be carriers for the condition that causes the loss.

The majority of people with vision impairments acquire them after birth, often as the result of disease, injury, or some other problem. For example, the most common cause of blindness in the United States is *cataracts,* a clouding of the eyes' lenses. Cataracts can result from injuries or can develop slowly over time, as in the case of many older people who develop them and experience a partial or even total loss of sight. In some cases, cataracts can be treated by removing the defective lenses and replacing them with lenses from healthy eyes supplied by an eye donor.

Among the diseases that can affect a person's vision is cancer. Thirteen-year-old Ivonne Mosquera of New York City tells how a bout with cancer left her permanently blind:

> I don't ever remember seeing—what colors look like, or people, or anything. I was born in South America. I was living in Colombia with my parents and two older sisters, Sandra and Liliana, when I was diagnosed as having retina blastoma bilateral, which means cancerous tumors in my eyes. I was fifteen months old. My family moved to the United States a month later, just

In the 1950s, polio left thousands of victims permanently disabled.

> before I had the operation to remove my left eye. The doctors took out my right eye about six months later. If they hadn't removed my eyes, the cancer would have spread to my brain and killed me.

Impaired vision can be a difficult problem for anyone, but it is especially challenging for children. A complete or nearly complete loss of sight can markedly slow a child's development, causing him or her to sit up, crawl, walk, and even talk much later than a sighted child. According to medical writer Brian Ward in his book *Overcoming Disability,*

> Blind children need very careful training in order to move around without injuring themselves. Because their learning difficulties are so specialized, blind children are usually taught in special schools, where they can learn braille, a method of reading where the fingers read groups of tiny raised dots on the page.

Hearing Loss

Like impaired vision, hearing loss can be total or partial. Approximately one out of every 5,000 children born each year in the United States are profoundly, or completely, deaf, and as many as 10% to 15% have some degree of partial hearing loss that makes taking part in everyday activities a challenge. There are many causes of hearing loss. Some are congenital and others are acquired after birth. Congenital causes, which account for a majority of cases, can be either genetic or nongenetic. According to Dr. Stephen Epstein of the George Washington University School of Medicine, the factors that may produce nongenetic hearing loss

> are medical disorders such as diabetes [an imbalance of the hormone insulin], toxemia [buildup of poisonous substances in the blood], or an underactive thyroid [gland controlling metabolism] affecting the mother during pregnancy. Other factors are infections that occur during pregnancy such as rubella [German measles] . . . and syphilis [a sexually transmitted

disease]. . . . Another environmental factor concerns any drugs taken by the mother during pregnancy.

Hearing loss that occurs after birth can be caused by various kinds of illnesses, including severe ear infections, mumps, measles, and meningitis, an inflammation of the brain and nerve tissues. Parents Lewis and Debbie Cohn tell how meningitis caused hearing loss in their son:

> One summer evening, David, our sixteen-month-old, started running a fever. Due to his history of repeated

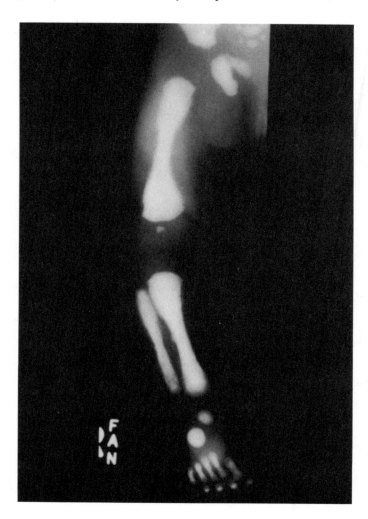

This X ray of an infant's arm shows that the child was born with a portion of bone missing

strep throat and bronchitis, I wasn't overly concerned. . . . [But] what I had thought was a simple infection turned out to be spinal meningitis. We spent the next three and a half weeks in the hospital. As David slowly began to improve, I noticed something was different about him. I couldn't put my finger on it, but I was pretty sure that he couldn't hear. . . . At my insistence, we called an ENT [ear, nose, and throat] doctor in for consultation. He performed some very informal testing on David and confirmed our worst fears. David could not hear. We later learned that hearing loss is a common side effect of . . . meningitis.

Learning to speak is much more difficult for profoundly or partially deaf people than for others. This is because people learn to speak by copying the sounds they hear others make. Because even moderate hearing losses interfere with speech and language development, they can and often do delay the educational process. As a result, many hearing impaired children get behind in school and never manage to catch up. Donald Meyer emphasizes the importance of dealing with this problem early, saying,

Deaf children often have very little speech and less developed social skills. Language skills are very important in a child's home and school life. So it is very important that young children who cannot hear learn to communicate through sign language or a combination of signs and speech. In order to help children who are deaf learn to communicate, parents, brothers, and sisters need to learn sign language too. Early medical treatment and education also help the child use whatever hearing remains.

Genetic Disorders

Sometimes certain incorrect combinations of genes occur in the developing fetus, genetic mistakes that cause disabling diseases and disorders. One of these disorders, hemophilia, does not usually display any outward signs of deformity or other handicap, and the vast majority

WARNING!

COULD YOU BE PREGNANT?

DRINKING ALCOHOL CAN CAUSE BIRTH DEFECTS

FETAL ALCOHOL INFORMATION HOTLINE

1-800-532-6302

This poster warns parents that unhealthy habits such as excessive drinking could cause birth defects in their children

of hemophiliacs appear to be physically nonchallenged. However, this is an illusion. Hemophiliacs lack a substance in their blood that is needed to make it clot properly, which means that they must be extremely careful not to cut or otherwise injure themselves. Even a minor injury can lead to uncontrolled bleeding, serious blood loss, and even death. Some hemophiliacs also experience bleeding into muscles and joints, causing severe pain and immobility. About 1 out of every 50,000 babies is born with hemophilia.

Muscular dystrophy is an inherited disease in which the muscles slowly become weaker. At first, a person with the disease usually begins walking with a waddling action, swinging his or her legs forward. Later, as the muscles continue to weaken, most physical activity, even standing, becomes difficult and the spine and limbs may become twisted and nearly useless. So, many people with muscular dystrophy must use wheelchairs.

A fairly common genetic disorder, *Down's syndrome,* affects about 1 in every 1,000 children and is most common in babies born of mothers past the age of 40. This condition occurs when one of the 46 chromosomes, the chains of genes inside each cell, is duplicated so that the child carries 47 chromosomes. "Children with Down's syndrome," Brian Ward explains,

> can be recognized by their slightly slanted eyes and small features. Some children with Down's syndrome have heart problems, and they are also likely to suffer from chest and ear infections. Children with Down's syndrome will nearly always have some learning difficulties, but some are able to attend an ordinary school. Others need specialized care and are educated in special schools.

One of the many other disabling genetic disorders is *Treacher Collins,* characterized by missing bones in various parts of the body. Francis Smith, a 16-year-old Indiana boy, explains about the challenge of this disorder, saying,

> I was born without a chin, and since I had no chin there was no place for my tongue—that just hung out of my mouth—so I had to have a tracheotomy [opening of the throat] in order to breathe. I had no palate—that means the roof of my mouth was missing, and that had to be repaired surgically when I was about six. I had no cheekbones, so my eyes were drooping because there was nothing to hold them in place. I had an operation to build them when I was about eight. For this procedure, they used bones from my ribs, because that's the one part of your body that will grow back again. I was also born without ears. Instead, I had what looked like two tiny knobs on either side of my head.

To correct this problem, I had five operations in which the plastic surgeon was able to make me a pair by using some of my cartilage from other parts of my body.

Other Physical Challenges

Many nongenetic conditions are also physically disabling. For example, some people have a developmental birth defect known as *proximal focal femoral deficiency,* more commonly known as an underdeveloped thigh. A person with this condition lacks the tissue in one leg to stimulate proper growth while in the womb, and that leg slowly becomes disfigured. After birth it can become difficult or even impossible for such a person to walk without braces or an artificial limb.

Rubella, or German measles, can cause many health problems in children, and the course of the illness must be watched carefully.

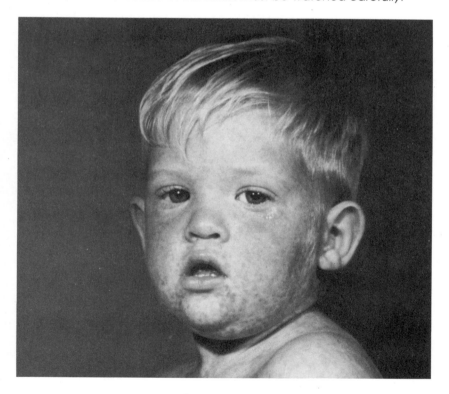

Some doctors think that certain drugs or medications taken by mothers during pregnancy can cause an underdeveloped thigh and many other disfiguring developmental birth defects. One well-known and intensely studied outbreak of drug-induced birth defects occurred in Europe in the 1960s. Thousands of women who had taken a new fertility drug called *thalidomide* gave birth to severely deformed children, some with no arms or legs. Just how many disabling birth defects are caused by drugs, environmental poisons, and other dangerous substances ingested by pregnant mothers remains unknown.

The most common developmental problem, spina bifida, which is Latin for "split spine," occurs when the spinal cord does not develop properly. Sometimes, the bones in the back do not close as they should to protect the spinal cord, and the cord protrudes from the opening in the spine. This causes problems with the nerves in the back, which can in turn impede or prevent activities such as standing up straight and walking. Some common side effects of spina bifida are extreme weakness in the arms and legs, paralysis, lack of control over urination, and hydrocephalus, an accumulation of spinal fluid in the brain causing pressure in and swelling of the head. Although a few children with spina bifida become mentally retarded, most have normal intelligence. About 8,000 babies are born with the condition each year in the United States.

A number of diseases and conditions cause loss of control over normal body movements and sometimes partial or complete paralysis. Cerebral palsy, for example, which affects about 1 out of every 500 children, most often results from brain damage due to lack of oxygen during birth. People with this condition can experience various effects, ranging from loss of muscular coordination, shaking, and unclear speech to extreme muscle rigidity.

Multiple sclerosis, or MS, is an incurable, progressive disease of the central nervous system. In the course of the illness, the outer coatings of the nerves harden and die, leading to numbness, weakness in the limbs, loss of balance, and often paralysis. Medical authorities estimate that at least half a million people in the United States have MS.

Another crippling disease, *poliomyelitis,* or polio, is caused by a virus that attacks the nervous system. Mild forms of the disease resemble the flu. But more severe bouts result in nerve damage and paralysis. Until the 1960s, when the Salk and Sabin vaccines became available, polio was the most dreaded of all childhood diseases, striking tens of thousands of people each year. Today, the disease is rare, but some cases still occur in children who fail to receive the vaccines.

Such conditions as MS and polio are not the only causes of partial or complete paralysis. Accidents such as falls, car crashes, and train wrecks, as well as injuries sustained on the battlefield in wars, often result in various degrees and kinds of paralysis, including *paraplegia,* or paralysis in both legs, and *quadriplegia,* paralysis in all four

A teenager learns to use a Braille typewriter.

limbs. Many people with paralysis have to use braces, walkers, or wheelchairs.

The physical challenges discussed in the preceding pages are but a few of the many that millions of people in the United States and around the world live with every day. Many of these individuals develop an extraordinary degree of courage that enables them not only to cope with, but also to fight against the effects of their conditions. Such courage is especially noteworthy when it occurs in children. Referring to physically challenged children she has interviewed and written about, journalist Jill Krementz comments, "Emotionally, they have an inner strength that has enabled them to fight and to keep fighting until they triumph over the odds against them. . . . Above all, they do not feel sorry for themselves, and they do not want us to feel sorry for them either."

CHAPTER 3

LIVING WITH A PHYSICAL CHALLENGE

To a physically disabled person, just getting around presents some daunting challenges.

As any physically challenged person can attest, living day in and day out with such a challenge is far from easy. Although parents and other family members are usually sympathetic, frustrations on the part of challenged and nonchallenged parties alike sometimes lead to tensions and hurt feelings. Many physically challenged people also have to deal regularly with cumbersome mechanical devices and other aids, such as wheelchairs and artificial limbs, that nonchallenged people never have to worry about.

The physically challenged also face social obstacles other people do not. For instance, it is often difficult for a person with a disability to find work or decent housing. Too frequently, this is because many workplaces, houses, and apartments are not designed to accommodate disabled people, or because some employers and landlords do not want to deal with physically challenged people. The situation is similar in many restaurants, stores, libraries, parks, and other facilities, which, despite laws mandating easy access for the physically challenged, have still not made the necessary alterations. Some owners and managers refuse to act until complaints, protests, or local officials force them to do so.

Dealing with Discrimination

This problem of nonchallenged people being reluctant to deal with or insensitive to the needs of the physically challenged is more widespread than many people realize. Unfortunately, some of the ignorant fears and uncomfortable feelings about disabilities that were common in prior ages still exist. Along with the daunting physical and often emotional challenges they face, many disabled people must also deal with out-and-out discrimination. Consider the following three true stories of the kind of discriminatory treatment many physically challenged people have had and sometimes still have to endure. The first, related by Gilda Berger, concerns a young woman in a wheelchair who simply wanted to attend a movie:

> The young woman and her friend got at the end of the long line outside the movie theater. The picture they wanted to see, "Coming Home," is a popular film about a wounded Vietnam war veteran, who is wheelchair-bound. The long line inched forward. Finally, the couple reached the box office. But the ticket-seller refused to sell the young woman a ticket. "Move aside, please," she said. "N-e-x-t." When she refused to

move, the manager was called. He was quite blunt. "Look, I'd like to sell you a ticket," he explained, "but I can't because you're in a wheelchair. There is no way someone in a wheelchair can see a movie here. The theater itself is up a flight of steps. Sorry, but you'll just have to leave." "But I *want* to see the movie," she replied. "My friend will help me up the steps. I'm in a wheelchair, it's true. But this is a movie about someone in a wheelchair." The manager thought for a moment. "Listen, lady," he insisted, "it won't work. The theater is crowded. There is no room for the wheelchair. I can't change the way things are. This building is just not built for handicapped people." Still, she refused to leave. . . . Grudgingly, the manager gave in at last. Through tears of pain and anger the woman paid the admission price and took her ticket. Her friend helped her up the stairs. She watched the film while seated in her wheelchair from a spot that the manager found for her behind the last row of seats.

In his book, *The Quiet Revolution: The Struggle for the Rights of Disabled Americans,* educator and author James Haskins quotes a young man who has also experienced discrimination because of being in a wheelchair:

Society in general is ill-equipped to deal with me. In the last fifteen years, my wheelchair and I have been declared a fire hazard in several theaters. I have been served meals in separate dining areas of restaurants since, as the owners were quick to point out, I might upset the other customers and lessen their enjoyment of the meal. On several occasions I have been very nearly hit by traffic as I worked my way across the street hoping to find a ramp or driveway onto the sidewalk on the other side.

Besides these blatant, physical kinds of insensitive treatment, many physically challenged people encounter a more subtle kind of discrimination. It consists of the common mistaken assumption that people with physical handicaps are somehow mentally disabled or deficient and cannot make their own decisions. The following narrative by Bruce

At the University of Washington in Seattle, people rally to support passage of the Americans with Disabilities Act. The steps in the foreground illustrate the problem.

Hillam, who must use a wheelchair because of a permanent injury to his spinal cord, comes from reporter-writer Sonny Kleinfield's revealing book, *The Hidden Minority: America's Handicapped:*

Once I went to a restaurant with my sister. The waitress gave me a menu but only addressed my sister. She asked my sister what I'd like to have, as if I were a baby. When something like that happens, I leave a penny tip. When I go clothes shopping, I need someone to help me get things on. The salesperson will always address questions to that person: What size does he wear? Could he use some suspenders, too? As if I were a pet. Two or three times a year, I'm stopped by religious fanatics who insist that I'm not up and about because of my lack of faith in the Lord. Or by the types who urge me to just hang in there, God has big plans for me. I was Christmas shopping last year when this woman who looked like a grandmother's grandmother came up to me and, before I could get out a word, she had her hands on my head and she was praying for me in the middle of the store. A really deflating thing is that many people equate a serious physical limitation with mental incompetence. They see my chair and assume I'm a dumbo.

Many Everyday Frustrations

In addition to discrimination, the physically challenged experience many other kinds of obstacles and frustrations in their daily lives. Some of the most frustrating times are those when parents or other family members, though well-meaning and sympathetic, have their own difficulties dealing with the situation. For example, different parents have different ways of dealing with the stress of raising handicapped children. Some parents become overprotective. They may feel they have to do everything for the child, even when the child is capable of doing many things on his or her own. Worried about further injuries, the parents may discourage a child who can walk with braces from leaving a wheelchair. Such parents may hinder their child from feeling independent and optimistic about life. Other parents may view the situation

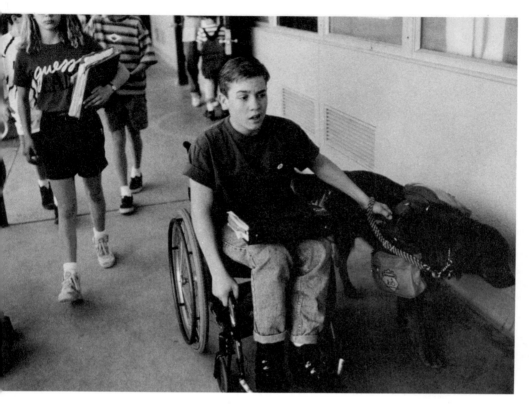

There is no reason why many physically challenged young people cannot attend classes at regular schools and participate in normal teenage social life.

as hopeless. They may become angry with the child, in a way blaming his or her handicap for disrupting the family, or they may withdraw from the child and treat him or her in many ways like a nonperson. Many physically challenged people live with one or more parents or other relatives who make them feel guilty, anxious, frustrated, or sad.

Although many physically challenged people have more positive and constructive home environments, they may feel uncomfortable dealing with friends and acquaintances at school, at work, or in public situations. The challenged person may feel self-conscious about his or her disability. And often he or she must endure almost constant staring by people unused to seeing someone with that particular condition.

Educator and medical counselor Linda Lee Ratto's book, *Coping with Being Physically Challenged,* quotes a young girl named Jennifer, who states,

> I was born with a cleft lip and palate. I've had two surgical operations to correct everything. Actually, I look pretty good compared to the pictures when I was first born. But I feel different. The way I look is okay. I realize that I don't have a movie star face, but I'm not ugly. But when I get in the middle of a new group, like the beginning of a school year, I begin to get those feelings. The old feelings that everyone is staring at me, everyone thinks I'm weird because my lips do not move over my teeth in just the normal way. Then there are the kids who ignore me altogether because they think I'm not good enough for them.

Many people who have physical challenges face the everyday task of having to use crutches, walkers, wheelchairs, artificial limbs, and all kinds of other special equipment. Besides the fact that this sometimes makes public access to various buildings difficult, using these devices can, in some cases, require unusual physical exertion, or even be painful. Using them can also be involved and time-consuming. This time constraint means that many physically challenged people are unable to get as many things done in a day as nonchallenged people do. Such devices, as well as the ongoing *physical therapy* necessary for some challenged people, are expensive, too. Although health insurance, private or government-sponsored, sometimes pays for part of these bills, many disabled people must somehow find the money to pay for the rest. "All told, I figured attendant care was fifty-two hundred dollars last year," said Bruce Hillam. "Wheelchair and equipment repair ran four hundred dollars."

Getting insurance of any kind in the first place is often another frustrating experience for the physically challenged. According to Hillam, his auto insurance cost one hundred dollars more than the normal rate simply because he uses hand controls for the car's floor pedals. Several companies refused to insure him, despite the fact that several studies have shown physically challenged drivers to be as safe

This new computer, designed by Dr. Edmund Gerhard of Germany, can be operated by acoustical signals and does not require the user to punch a keyboard. It is ideal for people who cannot use their hands.

overall as nonchallenged drivers. "And I had a devil of a time getting life insurance," Hillam added. "I only got it because of an influential friend. But I pay about a third more for my policy."

Finding Work and Housing

The physically challenged often have a similarly difficult time finding work. According to some estimates, as many as 50% of the disabled people who would like to work cannot find steady employment. Part of the problem is the practice of outright discrimination by employers

Today there is a greater recognition that the physically challenged can become active participants in the work force.

against physically challenged people. Other employers say they would like to hire handicapped people but cannot because their factories or offices are set up to accommodate only nonchallenged workers. It would cost too much, these employers say, to make the necessary conversions. Some employers claim that challenged workers have a higher risk of accidents or are less productive than nonchallenged workers. Yet a survey conducted in the 1970s by the United States Office of Vocational Rehabilitation found that the accident rate was lower for challenged workers in 57% of the companies surveyed. And the same study showed that challenged workers were consistently as or more productive than their nonchallenged counterparts. In addition,

This person, who suffers from cerebral palsy, is able to go on shopping trips with the aid of her wheelchair and a canine companion.

the study found that challenged workers in 55% of the companies surveyed had a lower rate of absenteeism.

And the problem is not only unemployment, says Gilda Berger:

> It is also underemployment. Many of the handicapped work in sheltered workshops, which are set up to provide undemanding work for the disabled—but at very low salaries, and with little chance for advancement. Even those who work in regular jobs often earn less than the non-disabled. For example, according to the 1970 census, 12% of the non-disabled workers earned below the poverty level. Yet 21% of the disabled earned below the poverty level.

This situation improved only very slightly in the 1980s and early 1990s.

Clearly, most physically challenged people find such difficulty in finding work and adequately supporting themselves and their families disheartening. A young woman with *epilepsy* summed up this feeling when she wrote to her congressman:

> It is my belief that productive work is a true good of life, a contributor to one's self-esteem, manufactured as we produce for others. For many years I have lived in hopes of being able to be a producer in my society. . . . I find in America, however, that the employers are still reluctant to accept the handicapped and let us build our self-esteem and produce for them. . . . I cannot do what I want to do most—WORK. What suggestions have you for me and the others like me who must be costing the country much wasted gray matter? Can't we be given an opportunity to contribute?

This difficulty in finding gainful employment directly affects the ability of physically challenged individuals to find decent housing. Because so many disabled people are either unemployed or underemployed, they often do not qualify financially for the loans needed to buy a home. And even those few who can afford homes frequently cannot move into them because they are not designed to accommodate the special physical needs of challenged people. Most builders automatically construct homes with nonchallenged people in mind, dwellings that lack such features as wheelchair ramps and easy access to light switches, faucets, and toilets. A study conducted in Massachusetts in the 1970s of the housing needs of paraplegics in that state found that 41% lived in inadequate housing. These homes were either substandard or filled with physical barriers. And 68% of those surveyed said that they would gladly move into better or more accessible housing if they could.

Experts say that the housing problem in Massachusetts is typical of other states. All across the country, in fact, inadequate work and housing opportunities regularly combine with such factors as limited physical mobility, barriers in public places, ignorance and prejudice, and the inability of family and friends to cope to make life for the physically disabled an ongoing and formidable challenge.

CHAPTER 4

THERAPY
AND TREATMENT

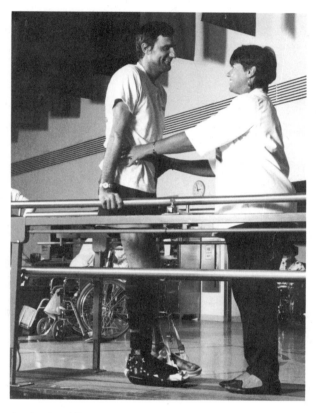

A physical therapist helps the victim of a serious injury learn to walk again.

Although most physically challenged people cannot totally elimi-nate their disabilities, many can and do respond well to various sorts of treatments and therapies. These forms of physical rehabilita-tion often make challenged persons more comfortable, allow them to be more active, and even lengthen their lives. "In most cases of permanent physical disability, however," comments James Haskins, "the individual's needs go beyond the requirements of mere physical maintenance. Interpreted broadly, the concept of treatment for the disabled encompasses training and therapy that will assist the individual in developing to his full potential, no matter how limiting or narrow that may be." In other words, the goal of treatment for a physically challenged person should be to make him or her feel as physically useful and emotionally fulfilled as possible.

Surgery and Prosthetics

Surgery is one kind of physical therapy that can help some physically challenged people. For example, as cited earlier, Francis Smith had a number of operations that helped correct some of the missing-bone disfigurements of Treacher Collins. Children or adults with severely curved spines sometimes have a *spinal fusion,* a surgical procedure in which a metal rod is inserted into the back to keep the spinal cord straight. Another kind of back surgery helps people with spina bifida. In this case, the surgeon closes the opening in the spine that characterizes the condition. Although the operation does not eliminate spina bifida, it can reduce the risk of infection and allow the person more mobility.

People with seeing or hearing impairments can also occasionally benefit from surgery. Certain types of eye problems, such as *strabismus,* or crossed eyes, can be partially corrected by an operation if it is performed before a child is six or seven years old. Correcting such problems later is much more difficult. "Only rarely does medical or surgical treatment cure children who are born hard of hearing," explains Gilda Berger.

> But some structural faults in the middle ear may be correctable. In the past few years, an operation known as stapes mobilization has helped to restore hearing to many people. In this operation, the surgeon lays back the eardrum, and with the aid of a special microscope loosens the stapes bone, one of the three tiny bones of the middle ear, from the oval window [passage leading

to the inner ear]. This is minor surgery that usually requires only twenty-four to thirty-six hours in the hospital and has a high rate of success.

Surgery is not applicable to every kind of physical challenge. And when it can be used, it usually does not eliminate all of the physical problems associated with the challenge. But surgery remains an important weapon

The buoyancy of water makes it easier for injured or disabled people to exercise their limbs and improve their strength.

in the medical profession's arsenal against some kinds of disabling conditions.

The use of *prosthetics,* or artificial limbs and other body parts, is another kind of therapy for the physically challenged. Although artificial limbs have been used for hundreds, perhaps thousands of years, earlier versions were crude, made of wood or some other hard material, and often painful to use. In the 20th century, large strides have been made in prosthetic construction. Today, such devices usually look and feel almost like the real thing and are much more comfortable to use. They operate through muscular or electrical signals from within the user's body.

Many disabled people have benefited from prosthetics, among them Hank Viscardi, a successful businessman and educator who was born without legs or feet. At the age of 26, Viscardi received a set of artificial legs. It took him a long time to learn to use them, but he persevered and eventually was able to run and even to dance. Viscardi went on to establish a school for educating children with serious disabilities. Ted Kennedy, Jr., son of Senator Ted Kennedy of Massachusetts, also benefited from a prosthetic device. At the age of 12, the younger Kennedy had to have his right leg amputated to prevent the spread of cancer in the limb to the rest of his body. He received an artificial leg and subsequently learned to walk, ride a bicycle, sail, and play football and baseball.

But artificial limbs are not necessarily the answer for every person missing an arm, leg, or hand. Fifteen-year-old Michelle Fernandez of Miami, Florida, for instance, who was born without a left hand, does not feel comfortable wearing a prosthetic limb. Michelle recalls,

> When I was younger, my parents treated me like a normal kid. Except they didn't want me to look different—not because they didn't accept me the way I was, but because they didn't want others to make fun of me. They wanted me to wear a prosthesis—a fake hand, which caused a lot of conflict between us because I never liked to wear one. It just isn't me. It took a while but my parents finally agreed that if I didn't want to

wear a prosthesis I didn't have to. Now that they've gotten used to the idea, they prefer to see me without a fake hand.

Clearly then, the use of prosthetics, although beneficial for some, must remain a matter of choice.

Physical and Occupational Therapy

Another form of treatment for the physically challenged—physical therapy—usually refers to exercises and other training that help muscles and bones become more mobile and useful. All hospitals have physical therapists who specialize in helping disabled people realize their full physical potentials. A therapist first tests a patient to see how well his or her muscles move and how strong they are. Next, the therapist plans a course of treatment that may include stretching or applying pressure to immobile arms and legs in order to help them to move better and helping the patient do certain kinds of exercises. One effective type of *therapeutic* activity consists of the patient executing a range of movements in a swimming pool, where the water supports much of his or her body weight and makes exercising easier. The therapist often teaches the patient how to do some of the exercises at home, too. In addition, physical therapists teach patients who need braces, crutches, prosthetics, or wheelchairs how to properly use these devices.

A number of different kinds of physical challenges sometimes respond to physical therapy. Among them are cerebral palsy, Down's syndrome, juvenile arthritis, and various kinds of spinal problems, including *scoliosis*—a curvature of the spine. People who have lost the use of parts of their bodies due to accidents can also benefit from physical therapy. LeRoy Hayman, a book editor and teacher, suffered severe paralysis in 1953 as a result of being struck in the head by a falling object. In his book, *Triumph! Conquering Your Disability,* Hayman recalled, with a touch of humor, some of the stages of his gruelling physical therapy:

Within a few days after arrival [in a hospital recovery room], I was lifted from bed to wheelchair and escorted down to the therapy "gyms." There, for exhausting hours each day, therapists mauled and manipulated, pounded and pummeled me, in hot water . . . tanks and on tables and mats, to revive my dormant muscles and nerves. They also taught and urged me to exercise myself. At first the therapists lifted me to a standing position, my legs braced with tapes. They then coaxed me into taking a few steps while holding onto a set of parallel bars. Later I [graduated to] a hot-water swimming pool, where a therapist worked with me. . . . I also rode a stationary resistance bike for at least an hour at a time, lifted weights, exercised with wall pulleys, and worked out on a rowing machine. I did sit-ups strenuously, as many as forty in a row without stopping. . . . In time I graduated from the wheelchair to crutches and finally to a cane. The improvement meant that I could now go home on weekends.

While physical therapy is mainly concerned with overall muscle tone, posture, and ability to move, *occupational therapy* concentrates on more specific and usually essential activities. For example, an occupational therapist often helps a physically challenged person learn to eat, dress, bathe, and use the toilet. Because these activities, once mastered, will take place outside of the hospital setting, the therapist usually works with the patient at home, in school, at work, or in whatever other setting the patient will frequent.

For a deaf child, occupational therapy can consist of teaching him or her to communicate with people and to take part in everyday home and school activities. Therapy might include instruction in lip-reading or sign language, as well as the use of visual stimuli. Lucille and Sydney Rattner used the latter approach to supplement other aspects of therapy for their hearing impaired son Steven. The parents recalled, "To encourage his use of speech, we made flash cards with words and numbers, posted the famous list of fifty nouns, and hung attractive *Saturday Evening Post* covers next to his bed."

Sign language helps deaf people to communicate. Here a teenager signs "I love you."

A Medical Team Player

Attitude plays an important role in all forms of treatment and therapy. A person with a positive, hopeful attitude who cooperates with doctors, nurses, and therapists obviously has a better chance of responding to treatment than a person who assumes a negative attitude and refuses to cooperate. Linda Lee Ratto calls having a positive attitude and cooperating being a "medical team player." She urges a physically challenged person to think of everyone closely involved in the person's case—the parents, doctors, therapists, and the person him- or herself— as members of a special medical team. According to this view, if it was a baseball team, the challenged person would be the pitcher. All

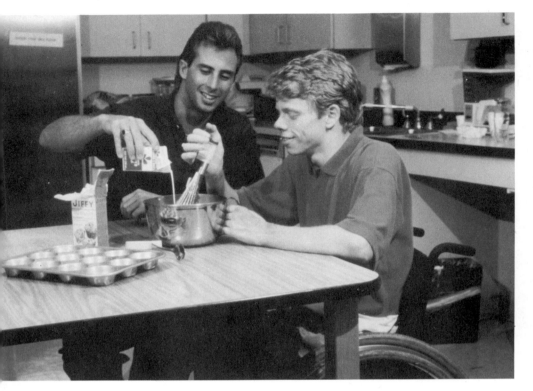

A physically challenged person is taught how to cook. Such skills promote independence and self-reliance.

members of a baseball team are important, but without good pitching the team will lose. Similarly, the support of parents, doctors, and therapists is important, but without the challenged person's positive attitude the treatment will be largely ineffective.

Ratto advocates the following steps in becoming a good medical team player:

1. Listen to your body. What hurts, what's different, what feels great? Tired? Sleep! Overweight? Watch the calories! Weak? Exercise, slowly at first, but do it!

2. Understand that every medical person is a person. He or she has a family, a job, and even gets sick sometimes.

3. Learn about your condition. . . . Read. Study. Become an expert on your disease, your challenge. You will understand the doctors better and gain a sense of understanding and control of your case and your life.

4. Write questions [you want to ask] in a special notebook you take with you every time you visit the doctor or clinic or rehabilitation center. . . .

5. When you have become good at asking questions, be sure to tell the medical people how you feel about certain things. . . . Say so if a new piece of equipment, such as a brace or prosthesis, does not feel just right. . . .

Physical therapists help a person to get the maximum use from weakened muscles and damaged limbs.

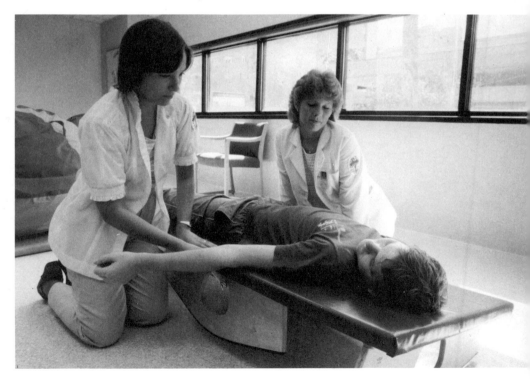

6. After a while, if someone on your medical team is not cooperative when you ask questions, consider getting another team member. *You* are the boss. *You* and your family are the ones who have to live with what the team does. . . .

7. If you find yourself firing your medical team, learn from experience. Go shopping for another doctor. Ask specific questions about the way he or she treats people like you. Don't be afraid to go to more than one doctor. . . .

8. COOPERATE! Follow the prescribed medications, diets, exercises, and other orders of the team you have chosen. . . .

9. Think of a visit with your medical team as a chance to learn as well as a time-out. Perhaps you can have a special breakfast or lunch before or after your appointment. Turn the day into an outing with the person who goes with you. . . .

10. Try to think of your office or clinic visits as chances to meet other people with similar challenges. Waiting rooms can be places to learn and make new friends. . . .

Using this sensible strategy will help maximize the benefits of whatever kind of therapy a physically challenged person is undergoing.

CHAPTER 5

COPING PSYCHOLOGICALLY

Sometimes the enormous difficulties that the physically challenged face produce depression, a serious obstacle to dealing with a disability.

In spite of the effectiveness of various treatments and therapies, most physically challenged people must learn to live with their challenges for life. And no matter how well a person adjusts physically to such a challenge, he or she also faces formidable psychological adjustments. As mentioned earlier, for example, a severe disability affects or alters relationships with family and friends. Other issues that have a psychological impact on a disabled person include dealing with depression, maintaining a positive self-image, feeling independent, fitting in at school or at work, and feeling comfortable about dating and one's own sexual identity. Usually, if a physically challenged person has been able to deal successfully with most or all of these issues, in addition to the purely physical aspects of the condition, he or she can, in effect, manage to overcome the challenge. The result can be a useful, happy life that fulfills the person's personal potential.

Fighting Trauma and Depression

Many physically challenged people, especially those that acquire their challenges rather suddenly as the result of accident or disease, undergo some degree of *trauma*. Trauma is a disordered mental state or behavior that results from severe emotional stress or physical injury. The sweeping changes in a person's life brought on by a physical challenge may be too much for the person to cope with at first. So he or she may react to this increased stress by becoming depressed, crying a lot, or verbally abusing or even withdrawing from family and friends. The severity of trauma depends on the individual and on how many demands are placed upon him or her. "Take for example," say DeLoach and Greer,

> the adjustive demands placed on an individual who loses his sight. These demands are physical—learning Braille or how to use a white cane or guide dog; psychological—altering assumptions of reality to incorporate the fact of a permanent disability; and social—developing new interests involving friends [and family]. . . . Disability-related stress might be greater for someone who is told that his blindness is permanent, caused by a malignant tumor, and whose fiancee breaks their engagement than for someone who is told that he might recover some vision and whose fiancee is supportive. Nevertheless, it is impossible to predict any individual's reaction with total accuracy.

After the accident that paralyzed him and turned his life upside-down, LeRoy Hayman went through a period of emotional trauma, followed by feelings of depression he calls "the blues." This is a normal and understandable reaction, he says.

> You sometimes feel that you've been cheated, that you've been denied certain human rights that others your age . . . or older or younger, take for granted. . . . And frankly you're envious. You can't do the physical things they do, and the blues, the midnight blues, sometimes take over. The blues, those melancholy feelings, are often visible in your unhappy face and slumping body. And the result is that many people who see you feel sorry for you. They pity you. But pity is just what you don't want or need, for it doesn't help you one little bit. Pity only gets down in the pits with you, wallows in the mud with you.

To counteract the feelings of depression, pity, and despair, Hayman suggests developing a positive attitude and self-image. The challenged person should realize that he or she is capable, self-reliant, and in control, he says. The person should learn to appreciate the facts of being alive, having a functioning, clear-thinking brain, and being capable of giving and receiving love. This kind of positive, forward-looking thinking, Hayman advocates, leads to a kind of mental control that ultimately helps the person overcome the challenge. In one sense, Hayman states,

> A physical handicap, however severe, is no handicap at all—as long as it remains only physical. As long as disabled persons keep control of their thinking and feelings, they can somehow cope with their disabilities. If the mind remains clear, if emotions do not govern, a person can survive—with some assistance, of course—all but the most death-dealing affliction.

Self-Image and Independence

Experts say that building the kind of positive self-image Hayman describes can be achieved by focusing one's energies each day on certain objectives. First, begin each day fresh, with the idea that

Unable to use his hands, this artist has found another way to continue painting.

anything sad or negative that might have happened the day before is now in the past. The new day will be better. One should tell him- or herself at least once a day that he or she is a unique and worthwhile person. Each individual's brain is capable of complex, useful, inventive, and often wonderful thoughts, regardless of the physical state of his or her body. In and of themselves, these thoughts have worth and potential equal to those of any nonchallenged person. And each day try doing, reading about, or thinking about something new. This way one is constantly challenged with fresh experiences and ideas.

Another part of building a positive self-image is coming to realize that it does not matter what other people think about one's physical challenge or one's lack of ability to do certain things. Many psychologists point out that when a person gets upset over what other people think and say, he or she can begin to show irritation and anger towards others. This only serves to make things worse, because treating people negatively usually results in people returning that negative treatment. Showing others that one is content with one's own situation and seeks only to be treated like everyone else is more likely to gain the respect and friendship of others.

Eventually, once a person has built a healthy self-image, he or she will be better able to deal with whatever physical challenge he or she possesses. The person will have a clear idea of who he or she is—more as a unique human being than as a handicapped individual. A young man named Seth, who is a hemophiliac, has come to grips with who he is and what it takes in his life to make him happy. "At seventeen," he says,

> I've finally figured it out: I'm basically a loner. I love reading. I look things up, research things. I keep interesting information in my own two-drawer filing cabinet. I know more about hemophilia than any senior in my 900-student class. It's my disease. I bleed and can't stop sometimes. But you know, on an average day I don't even think about my disease. I have two best friends. That's all. I don't need any more. When they're not with me, I just do my own stuff. They understand me. I don't have to be bothered explaining myself over and over. I know my buddies like me. I really like them too. Our being friends has helped me learn that I'm a great guy in my own way. Now, even when I'm by myself, I'm happy.

Obviously, Seth's successful development of a healthy self-image has allowed him to become as independent in both his activities and his thinking as any nonchallenged person. He has learned to rely on himself rather than on others in most situations. However, sooner or later, even the most independent physically challenged person must,

Special large-print books make a great deal of literature available to people with weakened eyesight.

because of his or her special challenge, seek and accept help from doctors, parents, or spouses. This does not mean that the challenged person is becoming dependent again. After all, everyone, challenged and nonchallenged alike, needs a helping hand from time to time. Nevertheless, for many physically challenged people accepting help is a reminder that they cannot deal with their challenge completely alone. "Disabled people know that there are inevitably occasions when they will need help, but that does not mean that they have to like it," writes Peter White, producer of TV programs about the physically challenged, in his book *Disabled People*. White continues:

> Many people have worked hard for the independence they have, and it is difficult to accept that there are still times when they have to put the control of their life into the hands of someone else, however briefly. . . . Most disabled people have learned to accept help gracefully, but occasionally the halo will slip and rudeness, born of frustration, may follow. If a disabled person is rude to you, there is no earthly reason why you should not be rude back. After all, being justifiably angry at a disabled person is part of treating him or her as normal and capable.

Having a Love Life

Most physically challenged people agree that feelings of independence and of being normal and capable are enhanced when they can enjoy a social life, especially a love life. For young people this means dating. For older and married people it means more intimate relations. Many people mistakenly assume that most of the physically challenged are either disinterested in or incapable of dating or engaging in sex. This myth has been perpetuated over the years by stereotypes of unmarried, celibate, or asexual disabled people in popular books, plays, and movies. Also, in past eras a large number of the physically challenged remained shut-ins in homes and institutions and therefore rarely had the opportunity to meet people and have relationships. According to DeLoach and Greer,

> Before sexual freedom and equal rights for the handi-
> capped became social movements [in the 1960s and
> 1970s], the sexual relationships of disabled individu-
> als were private affairs without influence on public
> attitudes or policies. Thirty years ago . . . one seldom
> saw disabled people engaged in everyday activities.
> Because most did not mingle with persons outside of
> their families or institutional settings, they had little
> opportunity to meet, court, and marry. Therefore, with
> little opportunity to be sexually active, such persons
> were considered incapable of sexual activity.

However, physically challenged people want, need, and deserve to
have intimate relationships the same way nonchallenged people do.
Some challenged people have difficulty at first in finding someone they
are comfortable with or who is comfortable with them. Confesses a
young man named Joshua,

> I have had a very hard time dating. I was born with
> spina bifida. . . . A lot of girls I ask out get an impatient
> look in their eyes, or they look around because they're
> embarrassed to be seen with me. I wish they'd forget
> other people and get to know me. . . . Now that I'm
> turning eighteen next week, I've decided to . . . go out
> with my buddies and their girls, or at least with one
> other couple. . . . I know whoever I end up marrying
> will have to have a lot of understanding and patience.
> I just haven't found my girl yet, that's all.

Joshua's optimism about the future is significant and heartening.
Despite his initial lack of success in dating, he remains confident that
someone is out there for him and that he will eventually find her. This
is an important psychological adjustment for any physically challenged
person, one that allows him or her to enjoy the same hopes and dreams
about loving and being loved as nonchallenged persons enjoy. Susan,
a young woman with cerebral palsy, has realized her dream. She recalls
that after she met Tim, a young man who also has cerebral palsy,

> I took to him straight away. It was a relief to find
> someone I could joke with and not have to worry if we

Group activities promote increased socialization among the physically challenged.

were offending each other; who understood all the problems; who didn't flinch when you twitched, probably because he was twitching too. To cut a long story short, we decided to get married. Mum was horrified, she still hasn't got over it really . . . but I knew it was right. We've managed to get a [handicapped-] adapted house and I am now expecting our first baby.

Inspiring Others

Challenged people like Susan, who have battled the range of psychological adjustments, managing to overcome trauma and depression, to develop a healthy self-image, to become independent, and finally to achieve success in dating and love, can look forward to enjoying happy, fulfilled lives. Not everyone lives up to their potential in life. This applies to challenged and nonchallenged people alike. But physically challenged people who are still struggling with issues like self-image and independence often believe that achieving that potential is harder for them, perhaps impossible. Success stories like Susan's provide hope by showing that such success is possible.

Even more inspiring are the stories of physically challenged people who have overcome all obstacles and gone on to achieve worldwide fame. Ludwig van Beethoven (1770–1827), for example, was one of the greatest composers who ever lived, despite the fact that he became completely deaf in his young adulthood. Locked in what he considered a prison of silence, he was able to hear music only in his own mind. Yet Beethoven refused to be defeated by this challenge. He went on to produce many great works, including his ninth symphony, perhaps the most sublime musical piece ever written.

Helen Keller (1880–1968), struck totally blind and deaf at the age of 19 months, could not communicate with others in her early childhood and was considered by most experts to be unteachable. Then a teacher of the deaf, Anne Sullivan, began working with Helen. After much difficulty and frustration, Sullivan finally succeeded in showing the child the connection between words and objects by spelling out the word "water" in Helen's hand while letting her feel the flow of water from a fountain on the other hand. Helen Keller went on not only to communicate, but also to become a college graduate, author, lecturer, and inspiration to physically challenged people everywhere. Never forgetting that wonderful moment beside the fountain, Keller later wrote,

> Once I knew only darkness and stillness. . . . My life was without past or future. . . . But a little word from the fingers of another fell into my hand that clutched at emptiness, and my heart leaped to the rapture of living.

Perhaps no other physically challenged person has gained as much fame and power as Franklin Delano Roosevelt (1882–1945). In 1921, at the age of 39, Roosevelt contracted polio, and his legs became permanently paralyzed. Confined to a wheelchair and able to walk only with steel braces and the help of a companion, he overcame fear, depression, and despair and decided to pursue his political career in spite of his challenge. "Once I spent two years in bed trying to move my big toe," he said later. "After that, everything seems easy." Roosevelt went on to serve two terms as governor of New York State and then won election as president of the United States four times in a row,

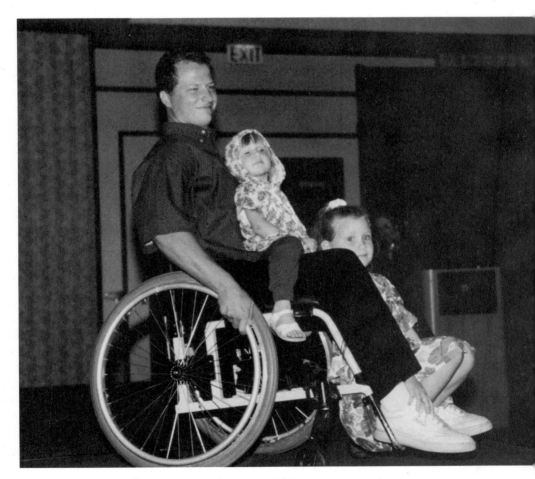

The support of family groups, particularly children, can go a long way toward easing the burden on the physically challenged.

valiantly leading the country through the horrors of the Great Depression and World War II. He became a symbol of strength and courage and millions around the world wept openly when he died in 1945.

Many other physically challenged people have become well-known achievers. The French painter Henri de Toulouse-Lautrec had malformed legs that gave him a dwarflike stature, and singers Ray Charles and Stevie Wonder are blind. Actors Sammy Davis, Jr., and Rex Harrison had only one eye, as does actor Peter Falk. Oscar-winning actress Marlee Matlin is deaf. The famous concert violinist Itzhak Perlman, paralyzed as a result of polio, is one of the most sought-after musicians in the world, and the brilliant physicist Stephen Hawking, paralyzed by *Lou Gehrig's disease,* continues to help revolutionize human knowledge about the way the universe works. These and many other people who have courageously overcome both the physical and psychological barriers of a physical challenge remain an inspiration to everyone.

CHAPTER 6

COMPETING IN SPORTS AND GAMES

Paraplegic Karen Jacobs, fastened to her instructor, tries skydiving.

In the last few decades, taking part in various kinds of athletics has greatly helped many physically challenged individuals to realize their personal potentials. Competition in a wide range of sports and games has proven to be therapeutic, both physically and psychologically, allowing the participants to feel the thrill and satisfaction of accomplishment. Such competition also creates an atmosphere in which challenged people can meet and become friends with others with similar backgrounds. In addition, as those involved will attest, these contests are just plain fun.

If nothing else, taking part in athletics is a way for physically challenged people to stay in good physical condition. Often, such individuals feel that because they have a lifelong physical limitation it means they are somehow exempted from staying in shape. This could not be further from the truth. "It's our responsibility, and no one else's," advocates LeRoy Hayman,

> to preserve, maintain, and develop what we still have.
> . . . Even if your disability keeps you permanently in
> the sack or in a wheelchair, you've still got to exercise.
> "If you don't use it, you'll lose it." That's a glib
> remark, but it is also true. You've got to keep moving,
> however slowly and painfully, until almost every part
> of your body has had its moment of exertion. Check
> with your doctor for an exercise program to fit your
> individual needs.

For those with the most severe physical limitations, the only exertion possible may be a set of daily exercises, perhaps in bed, in a heated pool, or elsewhere. Depending on the individual and his on her degree of limitation, such exercises might be done alone or with the aid of a therapist or family member. For many other physically challenged persons with less severe limitations, however—even those in wheelchairs—a wide world of sports and games awaits.

From Cong Fu to Wheelchair Olympics

Although widespread sports programs for the physically challenged are a 20th-century development, therapeutic exercises and athletics were used in several ancient societies both to help the sick get well and to prevent well people from getting sick in the first place. As early as 1500 B.C., for example, the ancient Chinese devised a series of light exercises called Cong Fu. The modern, more highly developed version, which also includes modes of self-defense, is usually referred to as kung fu. According to physical fitness expert D. B. Van Dalen,

> The Chinese believed that disease derived from bodily inactivity. To prolong human life, mild forms of medical gymnastics were derived. These exercises were a combination of stretching and breathing to maintain organic function. The medical gymnastics were usually performed in a sitting or kneeling position.

The Greeks, who were highly preoccupied with health and athletics, also advocated the use of exercise to maintain good health. Hip-

A group of quadriplegics playing their own version of rugby, which can get quite rough.

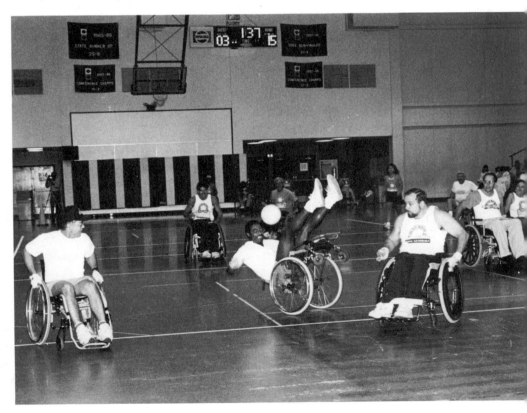

pocrates, later called the "father of medicine," wrote in his book *On Articulations,* "The wasting of the fleshy [muscle] parts is greatest in those cases in which the patient keeps the limb up and does not exercise it. Those who practice walking have the least atrophy [weakened muscles]." Hippocrates and other Greek physicians prescribed walking and other regular exercises to keep the body in good running order. The Romans built upon some of the Greek ideas about therapeutic exercise. The third century A.D. Roman physician Caelius Aurelianus, for example, had arthritic patients squeeze balls of wax to help strengthen their crippled hands.

One of the modern pioneers of therapeutic exercises and athletics was French medical expert Joseph-Clement Tissot. Beginning in 1780, he established the principles of modern occupational therapy and also introduced the idea of playing various sports as "recreational" therapy. In the 19th century, Sweden's Per Henrik Ling advocated the use of gymnastic exercises and sports for the physically disabled. He classifies such activities under three headings: those exercises the patient does him- or herself, those done to the patient by someone else, and those done by both patient and therapist together.

In the 20th century, the large numbers of disabled people produced by World Wars I and II prompted modern doctors to expand upon earlier ideas about therapeutic exercise. *Adapted sports,* that is, regular athletic events modified so that disabled people can participate, became increasingly popular among *amputees,* paraplegics, and other disabled veterans in the early 1940s during World War II. After the war, adapted sports became more organized. As Ronald C. Adams put it in his book *Games, Sports and Exercises for the Physically Handicapped,*

> The program of wheelchair sports began at various Veterans Administration Hospitals throughout the United States. . . . As these veterans played, they adapted the rules and regulations of regular basketball to their own specific needs. More and more disabled men joined into the new wheelchair sport until finally several complete teams were officially recognized. Thus basketball became the first organized wheelchair sport in history. . . . There were from eight to ten teams in active

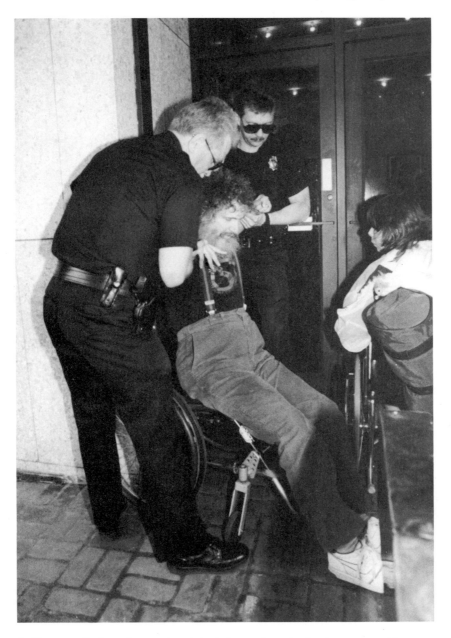

In Denver, Colorado, a wheelchair-bound protestor is removed by police from the entrance to a local hotel. He had been protesting the lack of access to mass transit.

competition in the United States in 1948. . . . Today there are approximately 30 to 35 teams in active play as members of basketball conferences and many independent teams. Each team plays from 12 to 20 games in an average season.

Wheelchair basketball received a further boost in 1949 when Tim Nugent, director of student rehabilitation at the University of Illinois, established what became known as the National Wheelchair Basketball Association, or NWBA.

At about the same time, the range of adapted sports began to expand, due largely to the efforts of Dr. Ludwig Guttmann of Stoke Mandeville Hospital in Aylsburg, England. Between 1948 and the early 1960s, Guttmann introduced archery, bowling, table tennis, shot put, javelin-throwing, fencing, swimming, and weight lifting for disabled people. And in 1952, Guttmann helped organize the first international games for adapted sports at Stoke Mandeville. Following this lead, the United States National Wheelchair Games were launched in 1957. In 1960, wheelchair athletes from around the world competed in their own version of the Olympics, a tradition that has continued and expanded since that time.

A Wide Range of Sports

Today, thousands of physically challenged athletes compete each year in a wide range of sports. In the United States, the U.S. National Wheelchair Games remain popular. Among the many track events at the games is the slalom. In this contest, the participants follow a twisting course set out on a flat surface and marked by flags, gates, ramps, and platforms. As the racers move through the course, their speed, dexterity, and maneuverability are severely tested. Other track events include dashes on a six-lane straight track and throwing the javelin, discus, and shot put. In these events, the participants are not allowed to raise themselves off their chairs as they perform.

LeRoy Hayman describes some of the other aspects of competition at the games:

Included in the swimming events are the breaststroke, backstroke, freestyle, and butterfly. All swimming races start with you, the competitor, already in the water. Bench pressing is the major event for weightlifters, and contestants are divided into classes based on their own body weight, ranging from light featherweight to heavyweight. Table tennis competition takes place under U.S. Table Tennis Association rules. Even quadriplegics take part in this competition. Because their hand grasp is weak, rules allow them to fasten the paddle to their hand with tape or a brace.

Archery is another popular sport at the games. Four contestants shoot at a time with coaches backing them up by holding arrow supplies and

In Florida, a group of physically challenged individuals trains for an International Wheelchair Race sponsored by Tampa General Hospital.

calling out the "hits." Various kinds of assistive devices are allowed, ranging from bow slings to help stabilize the weak wrists of competitors with cerebral palsy to amputee adapters to allow participants with hooks to grasp the bow and string. Even the partially blind are encouraged to compete, thanks to special telescopic sights that enhance the image of the target.

Cosom hockey, which became a sport for the physically challenged in 1967 at the University of Virginia's Children's Rehabilitation Center, is popular because it allows challenged players to experience the thrill of very strenuous competition. Another reason for the game's popularity is that almost anyone, with the exception of the most severely challenged individuals, can play. Although those without both arms cannot play a forward position, for instance, they can play goalie. The players can be either *ambulatory*—able to stand and walk—or in wheelchairs. Teams usually consist of four players each, including the goalie, who is allowed to use his or her wheelchair to stop shots. A game has three periods of 12 minutes each.

Some other adapted sports include riflery, badminton, horseback riding, billiards, and canoeing. Putt-Putt, or miniature golf, provides physically challenged people a highly competitive playing atmosphere with a minimal amount of physical exertion and risk of injury. On the other hand, three-track skiing, overseen by the National Amputee Skiers Association, requires a great deal more exertion. And perhaps the greatest overall test of physical strength and endurance for the physically challenged is the 26-mile marathon. Most major marathons held in the United States, for example the famous Boston Marathon, have wheelchair and other physically challenged divisions that attract literally thousands of competitors each year.

Low Organization Games

Some physically challenged individuals who enjoy sports and games lack either the physical stamina and mobility or the desire to compete in the active sports discussed above. And many competitors in these active sports sometimes want to take part in more informal games that require minimal activity. These needs and demands have stimulated

Where there's a will, there's a way. A one-legged skier enjoys a brisk day on the slopes.

the growth of low organization games, those requiring few rules, little or no equipment, and nonstrenuous activity.

Among the many low organization games is target tennis, in which ambulatory or wheelchair players use a badminton racket to try to hit a ball through holes in a wire screen. Another game, finger shuffleboard, is similar in many ways to regular shuffleboard, in which players use a wooden pole to push a disk down a long court and into premarked spaces to score points. In the physically challenged version, the players use their fingers to push checkers down a varnished piece of plywood. Another game, miniature tetherball, involves using table tennis paddles to hit a small ball on a string around a narrow pole. Games needing even less equipment include checkers, chess, and all manner of card games, as well as monopoly and other board games. Among the many low-impact games designed for severely challenged children are obstacle course, in which a child crawls, climbs, or pilots a wheelchair through a course made up of tables, chairs, and other readily available objects, and bean bags, in which players score points by tossing the bags into boxes set up at varying distances.

Whether strenuous or nonstrenuous, highly organized or informal, or stressing teamwork or individual performance, sports and games provide a healthy outlet, both physically and psychologically, for physically challenged people. These activities are not only healthy and fun, but they also constitute an important way in which challenged people can assert themselves, take pride in their achievements, and fulfill their personal potentials. Describing such benefits for a physically challenged player, Ronald Adams writes, "Essentially he wins recognition and approval from his peers at the same time that he satisfies his own curiosity about his ability to succeed. The result is a whole individual, in terms of his place in a peer group, since he utilizes his potential to maximum advantage despite his handicap."

CHAPTER 7

THE STRUGGLE
FOR LEGAL RIGHTS

More and more public institutions and private businesses are recognizing the need to increase access for the physically challenged and to punish those who ignore their needs.

Until the 1960s, the idea of fair and legal rights for the physically challenged was not a public issue in the United States. Indeed, most people were unaware that disabled people suffered any sort of injustice. Yet such injustice did in fact exist, as the physically challenged were routinely ignored, excluded, and isolated in many social situations. These people regularly encountered both blatant and subtle physical, institutional, and discriminatory barriers that nonchallenged people, out of ignorance, automatically accepted as the status quo.

Running up against these barriers were people like the young woman mentioned earlier who was barred from attending a movie because she was in a wheelchair and the disabled man who was forced to eat in a secluded section of a restaurant so as not to "upset" the customers. And there were also the thousands of handicapped people for whom everyday shopping was a harrowing experience due to vast, crowded parking lots, formidable curbs, stairways, escalators, and inaccessible public transportation and rest rooms. As James Haskins points out, society also excluded

> the man in the wheelchair who is unable to vote be-
> cause he cannot make it up the steps to the entrance at
> the polling place; the deaf child who cannot obtain an
> adequate education because there is no place for him
> in the public school system; the dwarf who cannot
> reach the dial on a public telephone; the one-armed
> man who is denied employment because he is consid-
> ered an "insurance risk."

Becoming Politically Active

Today, thanks to three decades of legal struggle by physically challenged people and their advocates, many, although not all, of these social barriers have been removed. This difficult and dramatic struggle began quietly in the 1950s when groups of disabled people and their families began banding together and forming special interest groups. Some of these included the Muscular Dystrophy Association of America, the National Federation of the Blind, and the United Cerebral Palsy Associations. These and other similar groups raised funds to support research, diagnostic clinics, and vocational training for disabled people. They also staged "walkathons" and "telethons" that increased public awareness of various physical challenges and the everyday problems challenged people face.

In the 1960s, inspired by the bold black civil rights movement that sought fair social and legal treatment of African Americans, disabled groups began to be more politically active. Physically challenged people started letter-writing campaigns to government officials and participated in sit-ins, wheel-ins, and other kinds of public demonstrations. They also took legal action, in some cases bringing discrimination suits to court. And representatives of many disabled groups lobbied Congress for laws that would make such discrimination illegal. Their voices were strengthened in the late 1960s and early 1970s by disabled veterans groups. Veterans who returned on crutches or in wheelchairs from the Vietnam War encountered the same kinds of injustices other disabled Americans had been complaining about for years. Angry over such treatment after giving so much for their country, these veterans joined the fight and demanded new laws protecting the disabled.

Slowly but steadily, the fight for legal rights for the physically challenged achieved success. One of the first pieces of legislation passed in this area in the 1960s was the Elementary and Secondary Education Act. Title VI of this act significantly increased educational opportunities for handicapped schoolchildren. In the same year, Congress established the National Commission on Architectural Barriers to the Rehabilitation of the Handicapped. This commission was created to study the problem of stairs and other barriers to the handicapped in public buildings and to propose ways of correcting the problem. The result was the 1968 Architectural Barriers Act. This act stated that "Any building constructed or leased in whole or in part with federal funds must be made accessible to and usable by the physically handicapped." This meant, for instance, the installation of ramps and wider doors for wheelchair access. Although they considered it a step in the right direction, many disabled groups criticized the act for not going far enough. It did not, they said, pertain to private housing or military installations.

Two Landmark Bills

The first great legal watersheds for the physically challenged occurred in 1973 and 1975. The landmark Rehabilitation Act of 1973 made

With specially adapted controls, this quadriplegic has no difficulty driving an automobile safely.

certain types of discrimination against the disabled illegal. Section 504 of the act stated:

> No otherwise qualified handicapped individual in the United States . . . shall, solely by reason of his handicap, be excluded from participation in, be denied benefits of, or be subjected to discrimination under any program or activity receiving federal financial assistance.

Section 501 of the Rehabilitation Act required all federal agencies to set an example for the nation by practicing affirmative action, or aggressive participation, in the hiring, placement, and advancement of disabled people. This meant that federal agencies had to actively look for qualified disabled people to fill open jobs, offer them on-the-job training, and make efforts to see that people who became disabled while on the job could keep their jobs. Because the 1973 law covered all employers who received federal contracts of $2,500 or more, it applied to about half of all the businesses in the country. Disabled people who felt they were the target of discrimination had the right to file a complaint with the Department of Labor. Between 1975 and 1977, some 3,500 such complaints were filed.

For many physically challenged people, the number of complaints only showed that the new law, although necessary and important, was not nearly broad enough. Like earlier acts, they said, this one only covered employers receiving federal money and allowed all other employers to continue discrimination. And ironically, the federal government itself, which was supposed to set a national example, was the target of many of the complaints. Unfortunately, because such laws do not immediately wipe out ignorance and discriminatory thinking, many disabled people who had been treated unfairly still found themselves in court. A typical case was that of Michael P. Zorick of Los Angeles. According to James Haskins, Zorick, who was an amateur wrestler,

> applied to the Clay County School Board in Florida for a job as a physical education teacher and was hired over the phone. But when the school board found out that Mr. Zorick was blind, the job offer was withdrawn. Mr. Zorick brought suit against the school board, and in October of 1977 Circuit Court Judge Susan Black ruled that the board was obliged to hire Mr. Zorick and allow him to "demonstrate whether he can satisfactorily perform the work of a physical education teacher."

Another landmark piece of legislation, the Education for All Handicapped Children Act, or Public Law 94-142, was passed by Congress in 1975. This act mandates that public schools must provide physically challenged students with a "free, appropriate education" in the "least restrictive environment." This means that all handicapped children are entitled to an education at public expense and in settings determined by the school administrators and the children's parents. These settings may include regular classrooms, special residential schools, or even hospitals in cases in which children need constant medical care. A set of learning goals, various kinds of special study aids—for example,

A sign alerts motorists to the fact that deaf children may not hear the approach of their vehicles or their horns.

reading materials printed in Braille for seeing impaired students—and scheduled meetings for parents and teachers to discuss student progress must also be provided. In addition, schools must spend at least their average cost per nonchallenged student on each challenged student. Public Law 94-142 advanced the rights of the physically challenged so significantly that many people refer to it as the "handicapped Bill of Rights."

Providing Sweeping Protections

Although the 1973 Rehabilitation Act and the 1975 Education for All Handicapped Children Act were important advances for the legal rights of disabled people, much remained to be done. No legislation had yet dared to extend laws protecting the disabled into the private sector, where many companies, stores, hotels, and restaurants still discriminated against them. After much political lobbying by disabled groups, a bill with sweeping protections for the physically challenged, the Americans with Disabilities Act, finally passed Congress in 1990. Writing in the magazine *Nation's Business,* journalist Bradford McKee remarked that the bill "amounted to a victory for disability-rights advocates in their long battle for tough legislation to make jobs and public places far more accessible to people with disabilities."

The bill has two main divisions, one in the area of public access and accommodations, the other in employment. The public access provisions, which officially took effect on January 26, 1992, state that all public facilities, including restaurants, theaters, and stores, must make "readily achievable" changes to afford access to disabled people. The exception allowed under the law is a case in which such changes would cause "undue burden" for the business or "fundamentally alter" the nature of the business's product or service.

The bill's employment provisions took effect on July 26, 1992, and affect companies with 25 or more employees. The minimum number of employees will drop to 15 on July 26, 1994. After that, businesses with fewer than 15 employees will remain exempt from the law. The law states that employers must make "reasonable accommodations" for job applicants or employees with disabilities as long as the persons in question are able to perform the "essential functions" of the job.

The Americans with Disabilities Act has so far been strictly enforced, and fines for breaking the law are stiff. A first violation can cost a business $50,000 and subsequent violations can be as high as $100,000 each. Between July 26, 1992, and April 1993, the government received 3,358 complaints pertaining to the law's employment provisions. Of these, 46% were claims that an employer wrongfully fired someone because they were physically challenged. The first company cited for violating the public access provisions of the law

A specially designed toilet for the physically challenged. Their needs must be taken into account by architects, interior designers, and builders.

was an Encino, California, firm that the government claims failed to hire sign-language interpreters for deaf students in professional courses offered by the firm.

Once again, say representatives of a number of disabled groups, the large number of complaints shows that many businesses are ignoring the law. This may be true in some cases. However, McKee points out, sometimes employers are either unaware of or unable to implement the act's provisions. "As late as [September 1992]," says McKee,

> two months after the bulk of the law was in force, 40% of small business owners responding to a nationwide survey said they were unaware of the disabilities act. An additional 30% said they knew about the law but could not afford the structural adaptations it requires.

Clearly then, despite much complex legislation passed to ensure them fair and equal treatment, some physically challenged individuals still encounter problems. Realistically, the new legislation, however sweeping and well-enforced, cannot succeed overnight in undoing the wrongs and neglect of centuries. Many older buildings, comprising the majority in the country, will have to make expensive structural changes, and that process could last for many years. And it will, no doubt, also take years for the outdated and discriminatory attitudes of many people to change. The physically challenged, who have made so many dramatic strides in recent years and who have been so patient for so long, still face an uphill battle against the painfully slow pace of real social change.

APPENDIX

A wide variety of physical aids and other resources are available for use by physically challenged people, and large numbers of people use them. For example, experts estimate that about 650,000 people in the United States use wheelchairs. About 690,000 people use walkers; 615,000 regularly use crutches; 205,000 have an artificial leg or foot; nearly 1.5 million wear special shoes; 400,000 wear a leg or foot brace; and at least another million use some other kind of brace.

But these very basic kinds of aids represent only the tip of the iceberg. With the advent of modern mechanical, and especially computer, technology in the last 20 years, it has been possible to vastly improve basic devices like wheelchairs and artificial limbs. Advanced wheelchairs activated by head movements and even by voice, for instance, are now available. It has also been possible to design and build special devices that allow disabled persons to participate in activities of nearly every description, including all manner of athletics, hobbies, art and music endeavors, and business and homemaking pursuits. Special bathtubs allow easy, safe access for wheelchair users; cleverly engineered exercise systems make it possible for partially paralyzed people to train at home by themselves; and hundreds of advanced computer systems and software programs allow physically challenged people to learn, communicate, work, and play. Following is a description of just some of these aids, along with the names of some companies that produce them. The addresses of the companies appear at the end of the appendix. The information was compiled by medical researcher and writer Richard N. Shrout in his book *Resource Directory for the Disabled,* a volume that should be consulted for a more complete and detailed listing of resources for the physically challenged.

Aids for Crutches, Canes, and Wheelchairs

ADVANTAGE of Torrance, California, makes storage aids for persons who use standard crutches, forearm crutches, walkers, or wheelchairs. Items include a crutch organizer, travel pocket, crutch bag, wheelchair side packs and backpacks, and an over-the-shoulder portfolio.

Travel on public transit, including airlines, can be made much easier for people who use the Ultracrutch, made by Luconex, Inc., of Foster City, California. The device weighs less than three pounds and consists of two telescoping blue aluminum alloy tubes that can be extended from a center section to fit all people from children to tall adults.

Fred Sammons, Inc., of Grand Rapids, Michigan, makes wheelchair accessories, including arm trays, slide-on lap trays, adjustable elevating armrests, side pouches and utility bags, clamp-on umbrellas, and Helparm, a functional aid for persons with impairment of shoulder muscles. This device has adjustable metal arms and eight pairs of slings that help to perform many productive tasks.

The Tote-A-Tot, a new, safe, and easy way to carry a child in a wheelchair, is made by HK Enterprises of Bemidji, Minnesota. The device offers a secure means for holding a child and allows the wheelchair user increased mobility for transportation and personal needs. The company suggests uses such as transporting, dressing, changing, feeding, napping, and playing with the child.

Ritterings, USA, of Denver, Colorado, makes Beachrings, which are 10-pound portable mats (10 by 3 feet each) that can be unrolled to allow a wheelchair to glide over the sand.

Household and Daily Living Aids

Alternate Stoneware of Charleston, West Virginia, a company started by a woman with impaired mobility, offers attractive stoneware plates and dishes for persons with the use of one hand, or with limited hand strength. Plates are made with rims that enable easier eating for persons with upper-body impairment.

Autolift is a special device for unassisted bathing. It lowers a seated bather into a tub by the turn of a handle that can be either self- or attendant-operated. Arjo of Morton Grove, Illinois, makes it.

Bruce Medical Supply of Waltham, Massachusetts, makes many household aids, including raised toilet seats, toilet safety rails, aids to make using buttons and zippers easier, devices that help pull up pants and skirts, pull off socks, etc., special jar openers, doorknob openers, and lamp switches with special grips.

Power Access Corporation of Collinsville, Connecticut, makes Automatic Door Opener, which attaches to existing door frames and plugs into a 115-volt outlet. The device operates with a remote signal, wall push plate, or wheelchair-mounted switch.

Fred Sammons, Inc., offers a number of kitchen aids, including knives and other utensils with special grips, an under-the-counter jar lid opener, and a one-hand eggbeater. The company also carries doorknob extensions, dressing aids, book holders, car door openers, and the Bed Reader, which allows a person to read large or small books in bed while lying completely flat or at varying degrees of bed tilt, as well as tools, writing instruments, crochet hooks, paintbrushes, crayons with special grips, and aids that magnify words and pictures for the visually impaired.

Directal, a special telephone operated by blowing into a plastic tube, is available from the AT&T National Special Needs Center in Parsippany, New Jersey. Blowing into the tube connects the paralyzed or otherwise mobility-impaired user with an operator, who then places the call. The company also makes an operator dialer, a device that automatically dials the telephone operator when the user touches any part of the device's surface.

Safe-T-Bath in Millbury, Massachusetts, makes Safe-T-Bath, a 5-foot fiberglass bathtub mounted on a steel frame that is several inches off the floor. The tub has a watertight 30-inch door that opens 180 degrees to allow easy access from a wheelchair.

Sports and Recreation Aids

Easy Access Corporation of Safety Harbor, Florida, makes the Multi-Exerciser, used for arm and upper-body exercise in a wheelchair. The company also offers the BedExerciser, which works the upper body of people confined to a bed.

Helm Distributing, Inc., of Polson, Montana, offers Nautilus and Nautilus-type machines adapted for people in wheelchairs. These can be used by paraplegics and quadriplegics.

The United States Association for Blind Athletes in Beach Haven Park, New Jersey, trains coaches and prepares blind athletes for national and international competition in both winter and summer sports. These include swimming, track and field, judo, wrestling, speed skating, and others. The organization uses all of the most up-to-date aids and equipment made for visually impaired athletes.

Information about athletic aids and competitions for the deaf is available from the American Athletic Association of the Deaf, Inc., of Burton, Michigan. This organization provides year-round sports and recreation opportunities for people with hearing impairments. The organization, which sponsors state, regional, and national basketball and softball tournaments, as well as training programs for coaches, consists of some 200 clubs with a total membership of 25,000.

Information about devices and aids as well as services and programs concerning physically challenged sports is also available from a number of regional and national organizations, including the American Special Recreation Association, Inc., in Iowa City, Iowa, the Amputee Sports Association in Savannah, Georgia, the International Games for the Disabled in East Meadow, New York, and the National Association of Handicapped Outdoor Sportsmen in Carterville, Illinois. Also see the sports organizations listed in the For More Information section.

Computer Aids and Computerized Devices

Adaptive Communication Systems, Inc., in Clinton, Pennsylvania, offers several computerized communications aids. The Alltalk is a human voice output communicator and training aid that uses a membrane keyboard that can be programmed in up to 128 positions. Voice output for each position is programmed by touching the position and speaking the desired phrase into a microphone. Words in any language, sounds, and music may be recorded and played back. Wheelchair-mounting systems, carrying cases, keyguards, and various picture symbols are available as options. Equalizer II is a portable communication and writing aid based on a portable computer with LCD screen display and built-in printer. A speech synthesizer is also included. Words and phrases can be either printed or spoken through the speech synthesizer. Especially useful for people with severe paralysis is Words + Eyebrow Switch, which is mounted on a visor. A lever projects down in front of the forehead, resting against it. When the user wrinkles the forehead or raises the eyebrow, the switch is activated. A small unit that projects a beam can be mounted on a pair of eyeglass frames, and the harmless beam is directed at the eye. Certain eye movements or blinking motions can activate the switch. One Screen is a software package that allows keyboard input using only head movement.

One-Switch Paintbrush, manufactured by Adaptive Computers in Albany, New York, is a drawing program for paralyzed users. The program enables the user to draw using a pointer in a way that simulates the feeling of holding a paintbrush. In the same vein, Dunamis, Inc., in Suwannee, Georgia, makes Leo's 'Lectric Paintbrush and Micro Illustrator, two excellent graphics programs that are easy for physically challenged people to use.

Arctec Systems of Columbia, Maryland, makes the Micro-Ear voice-commands system, a device that provides voice input for Apple, IBM, and several other computers. Type & Speak, a voice output program for the Apple II system, is made in Boston, Massachusetts, by Communication Enhancement Clinic. With this device, text may be modified before or after it is spoken.

A unique device used to play computer and video games, Mind Master is made by Behavioral Engineering in Scotts Valley, California. The device measures small changes in the electrical impulses in the user's skin and translates these impulses into a signal that activates the game paddle on the screen. No movement is required by the user, who simply rests two fingers of one hand on two electrodes of the sensor unit.

Craner Cabinetry in West Valley City, Utah, produces CompuDesk HCP, an adjustable workstation designed specifically for the disabled computer user. The main work area rises and lowers up to 12 inches in order to accommodate a variety of wheelchair heights.

Gregg/McGraw-Hill of Manchester, Maryland, makes Keyboarding for the Physically Handicapped, a touch-typing tutorial program for disabled people. The program provides the user with many options for combinations of fingers on either or both hands to be used during typing.

Isabel ("is-able"), offered by Magellan Corporation in Tallahassee, Florida, is a computer program designed for vocational rehabilitation counselors who work with physically challenged people. Isabel uses 95 physical and environmental factors to compare a person's physical capacities with the physical demands of 150 high-demand, high-growth occupations. This helps a handicapped person decide how best to utilize his or her individual skills in the workplace. The system works with an IBM-compatible computer.

Computer Foundation for Handicapped Children in Tempe, Arizona, makes Computer Aids for the Blind, a set of 21 programs designed for blind and deaf-blind computer users. Other companies that make fine programs and systems for the blind include Humanware, Inc., of Loomis, California, and Raised Dot Computing in Madison, Wisconsin. Among the companies that make systems and software for the deaf, including devices that teach American Sign Language, are Emerson & Stern Associates, Inc., of San Diego, California, and Microtech Consulting Company in Cedar Falls, Iowa.

FOR MORE INFORMATION

Company Addresses

Adaptive Communication Systems, Inc.
354 Hookstown Grade Road
Clinton, PA 15206
(412) 264-2288

Adaptive Computers
11 Fullerton Street
Albany, NY 12209
(518) 434-8860

ADVANTAGE
22633 Ellinwood Drive
Torrance, CA 90505
(213) 540-8197

Alternate Stoneware
P.O. Box 2071
Charleston, WV 25327-2071
(304) 346-4440

American Athletic Association of the
Deaf, Inc.
Martin Belsky, President
1134 Davenport Drive
Burton, MI 48529

American Special Recreation
Association, Inc.
John Nesbitt, Ed.D.
Recreation Education Program
University of Iowa
Iowa City, IA 52240
(319) 353-2121

Amputee Sports Association
George C. Beckman, Jr.
11705 Mercy Blvd.
Savannah, GA 31419
(912) 927-5406

Arctec Systems
9104 Red Branch Road
Columbia, MD 21045

Arjo
6380 West Oakton Street
Morton Grove, IL 60053
(708) 967-0360
(800) 323-1245

AT&T National Special Needs Center
2001 Route 46, Suite 310
Parsippany, NJ 07054-1315
(800) 233-1222

Behavioral Engineering
230 Mt. Hermon Road
Scotts Valley, CA 95066
(408) 438-5649

Bruce Medical Supply
411 Waverly Oaks Road
P.O. Box 9166
Waltham, MA 02254
(800) 225-8446

Communication Enhancement Clinic
Children's Hospital Medical Center
Fegan Plaza, 300 Longwood
Avenue
Boston, MA 02115
(617) 735-6466

Computer Foundation for Handicapped
Children
Don Peterson
2645 East Southern, A326
Tempe, AZ 85282
(602) 831-3519

Craner Cabinetry
3190 South 4140 West
West Valley City, UT 84120
(801) 966-1127

Dunamis, Inc.
3620 Highway 317
Suwannee, GA 30174
(404) 932-0485

Easy Access Corporation
885 Second Street North,
Building A
Safety Harbor, FL 34695
(813) 762-EASY

Emerson & Stern Associates, Inc.
10150 Sorrento Valley Road,
Suite 210
San Diego, CA 92121
(619) 457-2526

Fred Sammons, Inc.
2915 Walkent N.W., Dept. 636
Grand Rapids, MI 49504
(616) 784-0208

Gregg/McGraw-Hill
13955 Manchester Road
Manchester, MD 63011
(800) 334-7344

Helm Distributing, Inc.
911 Kings Point Road
Polson, MT 59860
(406) 883-2147

HK Enterprises
Route 6, Box 188
Bemidji, MN 56601
(218) 286-2652

Humanware, Inc.
Horseshoe Bar Plaza
6140 Horseshoe Bar Road,
Suite P
Loomis, CA 95650

(916) 652-7253
(800) 722-3393

International Games for the Disabled
Eisenhower Park
Tony Giustino
East Meadow, NY 11554
(516) 542-4420

Luconex, Inc.
353-A Vintage Park Drive
Foster City, CA 94404
(415) 377-0155

Magellan Corporation
P.O. Box 10405
Tallahassee, FL 32302
(904) 422-2752

Microtech Consulting Company
909 West 23rd Street
P.O. Box 521
Cedar Falls, IA 50613
(319) 277-6648
(800) 383-SIGN

National Association of Handicapped
Outdoor Sportsmen
Larry Holoner
P.O. Box 25
Carterville, IL 62918
(618) 985-3579

Power Access Corporation
Bridge Street
P.O. Box 235
Collinsville, CT 06022
(800) 344-0088

Raised Dot Computing
408 South Baldwin
Madison, WI 53703
(608) 257-9595

Ritterings, USA
7700 Cherry Creek South Drive,
Unit 6

Denver, CO 80231
(303) 696-1510
(800) 428-1333

Safe-T-Bath
184 Millbury Avenue
Millbury, MA 01527
(508) 865-2361

United States Association for Blind
Athletes
55 West California Avenue
Beach Haven Park, NJ 08008
(609) 492-1017

The following is a list of organizations and associations that can
provide further information on
the issues discussed in this book.

Advocates for Hearing Impaired Youth,
Inc.
P.O. Box 75949
Washington, D.C. 20013
(301) 868-7593

Alexander Graham Bell Association for
the Deaf, Inc.
3417 Volta Place, NW
Washington, D.C. 20007
(202) 337-5220

American Athletic Association for the
Deaf
10604 E. 95th Street Terrace
Kansas City, MO 64134
(816) 765-5520

American Coalition of Citizens with
Disabilities
1012 14th Street, NE
Suite 901
Washington, D.C. 20005
(202) 628-3470

American Diabetes Association
2 Park Avenue
New York, NY 10016
(212) 683-7444

American Foundation for the Blind
15 West 16th Street
New York, NY 10011

American Society for Deaf Children
814 Thayer Avenue
Silver Spring, MD 20910
(301) 585-5400

Area Child Amputee Center
235 Wealthy SE
Grand Rapids, MI 49503
(616) 454-7988

Arthritis Information Clearing House
P.O. Box 9782
Arlington, VA 22209
(703) 558-8250

Association for Children and Adults
with Learning Disabilities
4156 Library Road
Pittsburgh, PA 15234
(412) 341-1515

Bureau of Education for the
Handicapped
Office of Education
U.S. Department of Health,
Education and Welfare
Donahue Building
Washington, D.C. 20202

Captioned Films for the Deaf
Modern Talking Pictures Service,
Inc.
5000 Park Street North
St. Petersburg, FL 33709
(800) 237-6213

Center for Independent Living
2539 Telegraph Avenue
Berkeley, CA 94704

Center for Sickle Cell Disease
2121 Georgia Avenue, NW
Washington, D.C. 20059
(202) 636-7930

Clearing House on the Handicapped
Switzer Building, Room 3132
Washington, D.C. 20202
(202) 732-1241

Council for Exceptional Children
1920 Association Drive
Reston, VA 22091
(703) 620-3660

Cystic Fibrosis Foundation
6000 Executive Blvd.
Suite 309
Rockville, MD 20852
(301) 881-9130

Deafpride, Inc.
2010 Rhode Island Avenue, NE
Washington, D.C. 20018
(202) 635-2050

Disabled American Veterans
National Headquarters
P.O. Box 14301
Cincinnati, OH 45214

Disabled in Government
13453 Overbrook Lane
Bowie, MD 20715
(202) 426-0015

Down's Syndrome International
11 North 73rd Terrace, Room K
Kansas City, Kansas 66111
(913) 299-0815

Dwarf Athletic Association of America
3725 West Holmes Road
Lansing, MI 48911
(517) 393-3116

Epilepsy Foundation of America
4351 Garden City Drive
Landover, MD 20785
(301) 459-3700

Gallaudet University (liberal arts school for
deaf students)
800 Florida Avenue, NE
Washington, D.C. 20002
(202) 651-5000
(800) 672-6720

Handicapped Educational Exchange
11523 Charlton Drive
Silver Spring, MD 20902
(301) 681-7372

Helen Keller International
15 West 16th Street
New York, NY 10011
(212) 620-2100

Institute for the Advancement of
Prosthetics
4424 South Pennsylvania Avenue
Lansing, MI 48910-5695
(517) 394-5850

Juvenile Diabetes Foundation International
60 Madison Avenue
New York, NY 10010
(212) 889-7375

Muscular Dystrophy Association
810 Seventh Avenue
New York, NY 10019
(212) 586-0808

National Alliance of Blind Students
1211 Connecticut Avenue, NW
Washington, D.C. 20036
(202) 833-1251

National Amputee Summer Sports
Association
215 West 92nd Street
Suite 15A
New York, NY 10025

National Arts and Handicapped
Information Service
Box 2040
Grand Central Station
New York, NY 10017

National Association of the Deaf
814 Thayer Avenue
Silver Spring, MD 20910
(301) 587-1788

National Association of the Physically
Handicapped
2819 Terrace Road, SE
Apt. A-465
Washington, D.C. 20020

National Association for Retarded Citizens
2709 Avenue E East
P.O. Box 6109
Arlington, TX 76011

National Association for Visually
Handicapped
305 East 24th Street, #17C
New York, NY 10010

National Captioning Institute
5203 Leesburg Pike, Suite 1500
Falls Church, VA 22041
(703) 998-2400

National Clearinghouse for Human
Genetic Diseases
1776 East Jefferson Street
Rockville, MD 20852

National Crisis Center for the Deaf
University of Virginia Medical
Center
Box 448
Charlottesville, VA 22908
(804) 924-5656
(800) 466-9876

National Down's Syndrome Society
70 West 40th Street
New York, NY 10018
(212) 764-3070

National Easter Seal Society
2023 West Ogden Avenue
Chicago, IL 60612
(312) 243-8400
(800) 221-6827

National Foundation/March of Dimes
1275 Mamaroneck Avenue
White Plains, NY 10605

National Handicapped Sports
National Headquarters
4405 East-West Highway
Suite 603
Bethesda, MD 20814
(301) 652-7505

National Hearing Aid Society
20361 Middlebelt Road
Livonia, MI 48152
(313) 476-2610
(800) 521-5247

National Hemophilia Foundation
19 West 34th Street
New York, NY 10001
(212) 563-0211

National Hydrocephalus Foundation
Route 1, Box 210A
River Road
Joliet, IL 60436
(815) 467-6548

National Information Center for
Handicapped Children and Youth
P.O. Box 1492
Washington, D.C. 20013
(703) 522-3332

National Multiple Sclerosis Society
205 East 42nd Street
New York, NY 10010

National Society for Children and Adults
with Autism
1234 Massachusetts Avenue, NW
Suite 1017
Washington, D.C. 20005
(202) 783-0125

National Stuttering Project
1269 Seventh Avenue
San Francisco, CA 94122
(415) 647-4700

National Tay-Sachs and Allied Diseases
Association
122 East 42nd Street
New York, NY 10068

National Technical Institute for the Deaf
One Lomb Memorial Drive
P.O. Box 9887
Rochester, NY 14623
(716) 475-6318
(716) 475-6173

National Theater of the Deaf
The Hazel E. Stark Center
Chester, CT 06412
(203) 526-4971
(203) 526-4974

National Wheelchair Athletic
Association
3617 Betty Drive
Suite S
Colorado Springs, CO 80907
(719) 597-8330

Office of Handicapped Individuals
Office of Human Development
U.S. Department of Health,
Education and Welfare
200 Independence Avenue, SW
Washington, D.C. 20201

President's Committee on Employment
of the Handicapped
1111 20th Street, NW
Room 600
Washington, D.C. 20036
(202) 653-5010

Rehabilitation Services Administration
Switzer Building, Room 3414
330 C Street, SW
Washington, D.C. 20202
(202) 732-1398

RP Foundation Fighting Blindness
8331 Mindale Circle
Baltimore, MD 21207
(301) 655-1022
(800) 638-2300

Sibling Information Network
Department of Educational
Psychology
Box U-64
The University of Connecticut
Storrs, CT 06268

Spina Bifida Association of America
343 South Dearborn Avenue
Suite 317
Chicago, IL 60604
(800) 621-3141

Spinal Cord Injury National Hotline
(800) 526-3456

United Cerebral Palsy Association
66 East 34th Street
New York, NY 10016
(212) 481-6300

United States Senate Special Services Office
Senate Sergeant at Arms
The Capitol Building
Room S-321
Washington, D.C. 20510
(202) 224-4048

FURTHER READING

Adams, Ronald C., et al. *Games, Sports and Exercises for the Physically Handicapped.* Philadelphia: Lea and Febiger, 1972.

Anderson, Peggy. *Children's Hospital.* New York: Harper and Row, 1985.

Azarnoff, Pat. *Health, Illness and Disability: A Guide to Books for Children and Young Adults.* New York: Bowker, 1983.

Berger, Gilda. *Physical Disabilities.* New York: Watts, 1979.

Bernstein, Joanne E., and Bryna Fireside. *Special Parents, Special Children.* Morton Grove, IL: Whitman, 1991.

Boslough, John. *Stephen Hawking's Universe: An Introduction to the Most Remarkable Scientist of Our Time.* New York: Morrow, 1985.

Bowe, Frank. *Handicapping America.* New York: Harper and Row, 1978.

Calvert, Donald. *Parents' Guide to Speech and Deafness.* Washington, D.C.: Alexander Graham Bell Association, 1984.

Casson, Lionel. *Daily Life in Ancient Rome.* New York: American Heritage, 1975.

DeLoach, Charlene, and Bobby G. Greer. *Adjustment to Severe Physical Disability.* New York: McGraw-Hill, 1981.

"Developing Employment Policies for Persons with Disabilities." *Monthly Labor Review,* October 1992.

Donavan, Peter. *Carol Johnston: The One-Armed Gymnast.* Chicago: Children's Press, 1982.

Garland, R. "Deformity and Disfigurement in the Graeco-Roman World." *History Today,* November 1992.

Greenberg, Judith E. *What Is the Sign for Friend?* New York: Watts, 1985.

Haldane, Suzanne. *Helping Hands: How Monkeys Assist People Who Are Disabled.* New York: Dutton Children's Books, 1991.

Haskins, James. *The Quiet Revolution: The Struggle for the Rights of Disabled Americans.* New York: Crowell, 1979.

———. *Who Are the Handicapped?* Garden City, NY: Doubleday, 1978.

Hayman, LeRoy. *Triumph! Conquering Your Physical Disability.* New York: Messner, 1982.

Hull, K., and P. Hearne. *The Rights of the Physically Handicapped People.* New York: Avon, 1979.

Israel, Fred U. *Franklin Delano Roosevelt.* New York: Chelsea House, 1985.

Karolides, Nicholas. *Focus on Physical Impairments.* Santa Barbara, CA: ABC-Clio, 1990.

Keller, Helen. *The Story of My Life.* Garden City, NY: Doubleday, 1954.

Kleinfield, Sonny. *The Hidden Minority: America's Handicapped.* Boston: Atlantic/Little, Brown, 1979.

Krementz, Jill. *How It Feels To Live with a Physical Disability.* New York: Simon and Schuster, 1992.

Kushner, Harold S. *When Bad Things Happen to Good People.* New York: Avon, 1981.

Lonsdale, Susan. *Women & Disability: The Experience of Physical Disabilities Among Women.* New York: St. Martin's Press, 1990.

McCoy, F. "Disabilities Act: Cheers and Fears." *Black Enterprise,* December 1992.

McKee, B. A. "The Disabilities Labyrinth." *Nation's Business,* April 1993.

Meyer, Donald J., et al. *Living with a Brother or Sister with Special Needs: A Book for Sibs.* Seattle: University of Washington Press, 1985.

National Center for Law and the Deaf. *Legal Rights of Hearing-Impaired People.* Washington, D.C.: Gallaudet College Press, 1982.

Ratto, Linda Lee. *Coping with Being Physically Challenged.* New York: Rosen, 1991.

Schwartz, Sue, ed. *Choices in Deafness: A Parents Guide.* Rockville, MD: Woodbine House, 1987.

Shapiro, J. P. "Disabled and Free at Last." *U.S. News and World Report,* May 17, 1993.

Shrout, Richard N. *Resource Directory for the Disabled.* New York: Facts on File, 1991.

Siegel, Dorothy. *Winners: Eight Special Young People.* New York: Messner, 1978.

Stein, B. *About Handicaps: An Open Family Book for Parents and Children.* New York: Walker, 1984.

Sullivan, Tom, and Derek Gill. *If You Could See What I Hear.* New York: Harper and Row, 1975.

"Technology for Disabled Workers." *The Futurist,* November/December 1992.

Thomas, Andrew, et al., eds. *The Health and Social Needs of Young Adults with Physical Disabilities.* New York: Cambridge University Press, 1991.

Veyne, Paul, ed. *A History of Private Life: From Pagan Rome to Byzantium.* Cambridge, MA: Harvard University Press, 1987.

Viscardi, Henry. *A Man's Stature.* New York: Day, 1952.

Ward, Brian R. *Overcoming Disability.* New York: Watts, 1988.

Weisgerber, Robert A. *The Challenged Scientists: Disabilities and the Reach for Excellence.* Westport, CT: Greenwood, 1991.

White, Peter. *Disabled People.* New York: Gloucester Press, 1988.

Wilke, Harold H. *Using Everything You've Got.* Chicago: National Easter Seal Society, 1977.

GLOSSARY

adapted sports regular athletic events that have been modified so that physically challenged people can participate

ambulatory able to stand and walk

amputee someone who has had a limb or other body part amputated, or removed

arthritis a disease characterized by pain and swelling of the joints

cataract a clouding of the eye's lens

cerebral palsy a condition characterized by lack of muscular coordination, shaking, and unclear speech

congenital existing at birth

Down's syndrome an inherited disease caused by the body's cells carrying 47 instead of 46 chromosomes

epilepsy a condition characterized by seizures caused by uncontrolled electrical signals in the brain

genetic inherited

hemophilia a condition in which the blood does not clot properly

Lou Gehrig's disease a rare and incurable illness characterized by progressive destruction of the nerve tissues

meningitis a condition characterized by inflammation of the brain and nerve tissues

multiple sclerosis an incurable, progressive disease of the central nervous system that often causes paralysis

muscular dystrophy an inherited disease characterized by a progressive weakening of the muscles

occupational therapy exercise and instruction that helps people perform essential daily home or job activities

paraplegia paralysis in both legs

physically challenged having physical defects or disorders that keep one from performing some of the everyday tasks and activities others of the same age routinely perform; other terms used to mean the same thing are "disabled" or "handicapped"

physical therapy exercise and other training that helps muscles and bones become more mobile and useful

poliomyelitis polio; a disease, caused by a virus, which can result in paralysis

prosthetics artificial limbs and other body parts

proximal focal femoral deficiency underdeveloped thigh

quadriplegia paralysis in all four limbs

scoliosis curvature of the spine

spina bifida a condition characterized by an opening in the spinal column

spinal fusion a surgical procedure in which a metal rod is placed into the back to keep the spinal cord straight

strabismus crossed eyes

thalidomide a fertility drug that caused many cases of birth defects in the 1960s

therapeutic relating to or developing from healthful therapy

trauma a disordered mental state or behavior that results from severe emotional stress or physical injury

Treacher Collins an inherited condition characterized by missing bones

INDEX

Don Nardo is a filmmaker and composer, as well as an award-winning writer. He has written articles, short stories, and over 45 books, including *Lasers, Gravity, Animation, The War of 1812, Eating Disorders, Medical Diagnosis, Exercise,* and biographies of Charles Darwin, Thomas Jefferson, H. G. Wells, and Cleopatra. He has also written numerous screenplays and teleplays, including work for Warner Brothers and ABC Television. Mr. Nardo lives with his wife, Christine, on Cape Cod, Massachusetts.

Dale C. Garell, M.D., is medical director of California Children Services, Department of Health Services, County of Los Angeles. He is also associate dean for curriculum at the University of Southern California School of Medicine and clinical professor in the Department of Pediatrics & Family Medicine at the University of Southern California School of Medicine. From 1963 to 1974, he was medical director of the Division of Adolescent Medicine at Children's Hospital in Los Angeles. Dr. Garell has served as president of the Society for Adolescent Medicine, chairman of the youth committee of the American Academy of Pediatrics, and as a forum member of the White House Conference on Children (1970) and White House Conference on Youth (1971). He has also been a member of the editorial board of the *American Journal of Diseases of Children.*

C. Everett Koop, M.D., Sc.D., is former Surgeon General, deputy assistant secretary for health, and director of the Office of International Health of the U.S. Public Health Service. A pediatric surgeon with an international reputation, he was previously surgeon-in-chief of Children's Hospital of Philadelphia and professor of pediatric surgery and pediatrics at the University of Pennsylvania. Dr. Koop is the author of more than 175 articles and books on the practice of medicine. He has served as surgery editor of the *Journal of Clinical Pediatrics* and editor-in-chief of the *Journal of Pediatric Surgery.* Dr. Koop has received nine honorary degrees and numerous other awards, including the Denis Brown Gold Medal of the British Association of Paediatric Surgeons, the William E. Ladd Gold Medal of the American Academy of Pediatrics, and the Copernicus Medal of the Surgical Society of Poland. He is a chevalier of the French Legion of Honor and a member of the Royal College of Surgeons, London.

PICTURE CREDITS